ontokosta Winery
Vineyards
te

25

Orient

Orient Point

48

Main St

Greenport

Front St

Rd

25

Dering Harbor

Shelter Island Heights

114

The Old Field Vineyards
Mattebella Vineyards
Corey Creek Vineyards
Croteaux Vineyards
Onabay Vineyards
nnino Bella Vita Vineyards
phael
dar Vineyards
Cellars
ellars
neyards
ellars

Winery

Channing Daughters Winery

Springs

Powder Hill

114

Sag Harbor

114

41

Wölffer Estate

Scuttlehole Rd

Sagg Rd

East Hampton

Pantigo Rd

Amagansett

Woods Ln

Montauk Hwy

Bridgehampton

North Sea

Duck Walk South

27

Sagaponack

Water Mill

Southampton

D1154093

5 Miles

5 Kilometers

Atlantic Ocean

Long Island Wine Country

BEHIND
the
BOTTLE

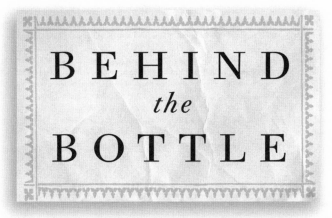

BEHIND *the* BOTTLE

THE RISE OF WINE *on* LONG ISLAND

EILEEN M. DUFFY

with a foreword by MARY EWING-MULLIGAN MW

CIDER MILL PRESS

BOOK PUBLISHERS

Kennebunkport, Maine

13-Digit ISBN: 978-1604335019
10-Digit ISBN: 1604335017

This book may be ordered by mail from the publisher. Please include $4.95 for postage and handling. Please support your local bookseller first!

Books published by Cider Mill Press Book Publishers are available at special discounts for bulk purchases in the United States by corporations, institutions, and other organizations. For more information, please contact the publisher.

Cider Mill Press Book Publishers
"Where good books are ready for press"
12 Spring Street
PO Box 454
Kennebunkport, Maine 04046

Visit us on the Web! www.cidermillpress.com

Cover design by Whitney Cookman
Interior design by Alicia Freile, Tango Media

Photo credits: pp. 24-25, courtesy Warren Street Books; pp. 32-33, courtesy Bedell Cellars; pp. 44-45, courtesy Bruce Curtis; pp. 54-55, courtesy Wölffer Estate; pp. 70-71, courtesy Pellegrini Vineyards; pp. 106-107, courtesy Joseph Reilly; pp. 132-133, courtesy Randee Dadonna; pp. 148-149, courtesy Lindsay Morris; 174-175, courtesy Warren Street Books; pp. 186-187, courtesy Paumanok Vineyards; p. 213, courtesy Doug Young; and all other images used under license of Shutterstock.com.

Printed in the United States of America
1 2 3 4 5 6 7 8 9 0
First Edition

Table of Contents

The Craftsmen

A Vision of a Sustainable Island

The Future of Long Island Wine

Foreword

Wine is fascinating for many different reasons. Some of us just love the way wine tastes, for example, while others relish the intellectual challenge of understanding the intricacies of grape growing and winemaking. But the human interest side of wine unites us all. To sip a good wine and hear the personal story of the man or woman who made it can bring that wine alive far more memorably than the perfect food pairing. And to hear the personal story of passionate winemakers is to want to sip their wines.

By bringing together the personal stories of more than a dozen people who grow grapes and make wine on Long Island, *Behind the Bottle: The Rise of Long Island Wine* enriches our interest in the wines that flow from these individuals' hands— and enhances our appreciation of those wines. Collectively, the stories have an additional effect: They weave a story of a whole wine region as seen through the eyes of the people who embody that region's wine culture.

The grapegrowers and winemakers whom Eileen M. Duffy interviews in *Behind the Bottle* believe fervently in the potential of Long Island as a world-class wine region. Many of them have relocated from far states and farther countries to practice their craft on Long Island and earn their place in the region's history.

Although each person's story is unique, they share passion and conviction for their region.

The author herself shares their passion. She has lived in Long Island's wine country for 14 years and has chronicled the region's wines and wineries since 2003. During that time, she worked to broaden her knowledge of wine by taking wine courses in New York City, which is where I came to know her. I was one of her teachers, and she was a serious and successful student.

Eileen's knowledge of wine and her fluid writing style underpin this book; she can clarify a winemaker's occasional technical explanation so it is understandable to less experienced wine drinkers and bring alive the personalities of each producer.

I don't know of a better way to get a feel for a wine region and its wines than to meet the people who make the wines. Through storytelling, this book will expand your appreciation of Long Island's wine.

Mary Ewing-Mulligan MW

Preface

For this book, I spun off a column in *Edible East End*, where I have been honored to work since at least 2005, called "Behind the Bottle." For each article, we would focus on one wine from one producer from a specific vintage year. It allowed us to write more than a review, because it included the inclinations of the winemakers, the vagaries of the growing seasons, and the history of winegrowing on Long Island. When approached by my patient editor, Carlo DeVito, about writing this book, we agreed it was a good format. Before I interviewed the winemakers featured in the following pages, I asked them to choose a wine they'd made that they felt was a milestone either for them or the region. It turned out to be a really good question; their selections told stories beyond the wine. I got history, weather reports, and tales of great accomplishments, serendipity, and friendship.

When interviewing these people, even though I have known many for years, I was impressed by the connectedness and six degrees of separation among all the players. Building a new wine region is a momentous task. There's so much that you don't know that you don't know, but every day you're still up at the crack of dawn to check if your vines have frozen overnight or if it has gotten hot enough, or cold enough, to stop the fermentation of grapes you've been rearing for a year, thus destructing a vintage's worth of saleable material.

If there's one thing I've learned at *Edible*, it's that, more than ever, our readers want to know who is making their wine or food. How good it tastes or how sustainable it is is as important as the stories of the people who make it. We want to know who is tilling the land that produces our asparagus, how they got into the business, and what they do each day. I never knew a farmer until I moved to the East End. Everyone I knew, including my father, brother, and sister and nearly everyone else in my high school, went into finance or worked in an office building. I ended up being the weird one, and I'm not that weird (relatively). Farmers aren't weirdos, but their lives are so different from what many people in New York's tri-state area can understand. If that gap of understanding can be somewhat filled by the stories in this book—about shy plant geeks, later-in-life career changers, and just plain pioneers—then we all can be closer to the land and our food and our wine, a beverage that has sustained through the ages and hopefully will outlive soda. Here's to your health.

Introduction

The East End of Long Island is really one of the most beautiful places. The steel-gray Atlantic Ocean pushes up against the shores of the Hamptons, where "city people," as the locals call them, have built fantastic homes and hold even better parties. Travel a few miles inland, and you'll hit an agricultural belt supported by what is called Bridgehampton loam. Generations of potato farmers used this now very valuable land to make a living that increased once the Long Island Rail Road made it to Greenport, on the East End's North Fork, in 1844, and to the Hamptons in 1870.

North of the Bridgehampton loam are woods in which herds of deer used to stay out of sight. Much of those woods are gone and now filled with houses; the deer eat the expensive landscaping.

Go north some more and you'll reach water again: the Peconic Bay, home to the tiny scallops that also once supported an industry. Smack in the middle is Shelter Island; sheep farms used to cover it. It's now a quiet rural residential area accessible only by ferry. Miss the last ferry and you're sleeping in your car.

The North Ferry takes you to the North Fork, where most of our story takes place. Bordered on the south by Peconic Bay, which technically has at least three names—Great Peconic,

Little Peconic, and Gardiner's—and on the north by Long Island Sound, the North Fork's growing season starts a good two weeks before the South Fork's. Potatoes and cauliflower once ruled here, but now greenhouses growing decorative plants and sod farms stand next to vineyards, which in the wine region's 42nd year cover 3,100 acres of flat arable land warmed by what wine geeks call a maritime climate. The bay and the sound have frozen only in the memories of few remaining old timers (there are stories of driving trucks to Gardiner's Island just off the northern tippy top of East Hampton, home of most of the working class) and in winter can be warmer than the air. This keeps the vines from succumbing to winterkill, which is good because replanting is expensive.

Though the bodies of water warm the vineyards, they don't actually make Long Island a warm place. Long Island's challenges and advantages stem directly from its clear four-season year. It's cold in the winter and hot in the summer; the shoulder seasons, as they are known in resort areas, are somewhere in between. Even given the erratic weather brought on by climate change, it's springy in the spring, when the region's vines break open their buds, and fall-y in the fall, when harvest starts around the beginning of September. This isn't to say the weather's predictable: It can be hot and humid, warm and wet, or cold and dry in any combination except the dead of winter— March is the dreariest—and the height of summer, when for a few weeks in August everyone's clamoring for air conditioning. In November the trees are bare and the snow hasn't started, if it will at all; it rivals March in drear.

In other words, this ain't Northern California where good weather is a foregone conclusion. A cool growing climate keeps you on your toes, but it also produces wine in the style of some of the most venerable wine regions in the world. Bordeaux, which butts up to the other side of the Atlantic, has to deal with rain during harvest, just as we have to deal with the threat of hurricane season in September and October. And we know they make good wine. Rias Baixas in the northwestern corner of Spain, just above Portugal, also borders the rocky cliffs of the Atlantic, and their albariño is famous worldwide. Germany isn't exactly a destination for sun worshippers, but their rieslings excel. It is an extremely short growing season in Champagne. New Zealand has a cool climate and so does Tasmania. I could go on.

In other words, cool climates are just as viable for growing great wine as the perfect Pacific-cooled vineyards of Chile or the sun-baked soils of Sardinia. They don't make better wine. They just make a different kind of wine.

In 2008, Stony Brook University organized a symposium called "The Art of Balance: Cool Climate/Maritime Wines in a Global Context." Among the guests were winemakers from Bordeaux, the Loire Valley, Germany and the Santa Rita Hills in California, where geography performs the trick of creating a cool climate south of Death Valley.

From the press release:

> For two days of talks, tastings, and net-
> working, participants will focus on wines
> with the unique balance, finesse, and energy

fostered by cool and maritime climate viticulture. The current consumer trend away from high alcohol, heavily oaked wines makes this symposium especially important for wine producers, aficionados and intelligentsia who want a better understanding of the more refined wines from cool terroirs.

What do you know? Seven years ago the wine community was talking about the same thing we're talking about today. Balance has overtaken fruitbomb in the race for ratings, high alcohol has caused nationwide palate fatigue and 200 percent new oak is now a joke.

But the press release, written by Louisa Hargrave, who was director of the now defunct Center for Food, Wine and Culture at Stony Brook, was more than a sop to a consumer trend. She had staked her livelihood on the success of cool climate wine on Long Island in 1973, when she and her then-husband, Alex Hargrave, planted 17 acres of cabernet sauvignon, pinot noir and sauvignon blanc in a former potato field in Cutchogue on the North Fork. Forty-two years later, she can look back at an industry that now employs thousands of people, draws 1.5 million tourists a year, and produces more than 500,000 cases annually; there are 57 members of the Long Island Wine Council, a trade group, and 35 wineries open to the public.

The wine council was founded in 1989; in 2005 a group of wineries formed the Long Island Merlot Alliance (LIMA), whose mission has evolved to promote Long Island merlot and merlot-based blends. The wine council is predominately a marketing and lobbying organization and has had a role in a number of recent changes to the New York State laws governing winegrowers and wineries that has extended to cider and beer makers. Recently the North Fork has seen a small farm renaissance, the younger generation of established farming families has been joined by newcomers who are raising livestock, making cheese, sprouting mushrooms, and growing hops. By last count, there are four craft breweries on the East End; five years ago there were none. Two years ago, there were no makers of hard cider; now there are four. The wine council's work with Governor Mario Cuomo and the legislature have made it easier for farm wineries and farm breweries to license their operations and sell their wares in more places without filling out multiple forms. In a boon to the many farm stands and farmers markets on the East End, a new law allows them to sell New York wine but not host tastings. And tasting rooms at the wineries are allowed to sell spirits and beer produced in New York. This a long way from the fall of 2005 when the State Liquor Authority raided one of the wineries and attempted to shut them down for selling crackers and bottled water.

New York State has had restrictive liquor laws, most of which are the product of the demise of Prohibition. Alcohol cannot be sold anywhere but a store with an off-premise liquor license, and those license holders are limited to one retail outlet. Restaurants hold an on-premise license and cannot sell booze to go. Both have to buy their wares from a distributor, and the State Liquor Authority will put you on the COD list if your payment is more than 30 days out. The Farm Winery Act of 1976, signed into law by Governor Hugh Carey, changed that. It allowed holders of the newly created farm winery licenses to sell their wares directly to the public as long as the grapes were grown in New York. This was three years after the Hargraves planted, and it added gas to the kindling of Long Island Wine Country. (The act also benefited the more established wine region of the Finger Lakes, which was revived in 1962 when Dr. Konstantin Frank planted his vineyard at Vinifera Wine Cellars in Hammondsport. Frank was a plant scientist from Ukraine who moved to work at Cornell University in upstate New York, and figures greatly in our story.)

LIMA has made research one of its focuses by hiring interns to study the aromatic properties of merlot and hosting visiting winemakers from other regions who walk the vineyards and taste in the cellars to share their experience. Many come from Bordeaux, where, on the Right Bank, they produce some of the most sought-after merlot in the world.

Long Island's cool climate allows a wide variety of grapes to grow. Even members of LIMA grow way more than merlot. Sauvignon blanc does really well, but so does chardonnay, which is more adaptable to winemaker influence like barrel fermentation and fermentation on skins. Like sauvignon blanc, other aromatic white varieties thrive here; it's a bit too warm for riesling, but gewürztraminer and viognier make distinctive wines with heft and zesty acid. Cabernet franc is an upcoming star.

Often used in blends, cab franc has recently taken a place at the top of the food chain with many wineries making single varietal bottlings. Its growing season matches Long Island's, and its distinctive herbal flavors and aromas—which can be derisively or positively described as "bell pepper"—take on a nuance when grown on the East End that makes for easy drinking, long aging, and complex flavors and aromas. Petit verdot, once also primarily used in blends to add color and tannins, is now being bottled on its own, showcasing the unique sachet aromas it picks up while growing here. I find it easy to pick out even when it makes up a small portion of a blend.

The trend at the beginning of Long Island Wine Country was to emulate the wine growing regions of Western Europe. Our original planters, the Hargraves and Dave Mudd, who has been followed into the profession by his son Steve, likened the local climate to Bordeaux, where cabernet sauvignon, merlot, and sauvignon blanc dominate. They also looked to Burgundy, where the plantings are either pinot noir or chardonnay. As it's shaken out, merlot and sauvignon blanc do very well, but cabernet is really only viable in the warmer western vineyards, which are further from the water. Chardonnay adapted like a golden retriever to a new family, while few wineries continue to place money on pinot noir. The exception is McCall Wines, which has been making a name for itself with its silky balanced wines.

A more forceful trend has been gathering around grapes from northwestern Italy. Channing Daughters on the South Fork started planting vines bearing pinot grigio, tocai friulano, refosco, teroldego, and lagrein in 1999. In 2013 Regan Meador, an ad exec turned winegrower and winemaker in a matter of two years, laser planted lagrein and teroldego on his property in Southold on the North Fork with the help of Steve Mudd. Meador wants to dodge chardonnay and merlot, the region's most planted grapes, while Channing embraces them as part of their repertoire.

As Mudd says he learned years ago from farmer John Wickham, after a day of hands-on learning, the most important thing—beyond soil, root stock, vines, wineries, and wine—is marketing. If there's no one to buy your wine, there's no reason to make it. So having a story makes a big difference. One successful example of this is Sparkling Pointe, which opened with the mission of making only sparkling wine, and they have done very well. Although the style is traditional—they only make wine from chardonnay, pinot noir, and pinot meunier, the three permitted grapes in Champagne—and their wine is made by Frenchman Gilles Martin, for Long Island it was something new, drawing crowds that return because the wine is good.

Mudd helped the owners of Sparkling Pointe decide what to plant and connected them with Martin. This is one small example of the importance of growers in any wine region. Growers not only tend their own vineyards, they manage the vineyards of others. This means they are a social lot; while winemakers are mostly stuck among barrels, tanks, and bottling lines, winegrowers are driving around, talking to everyone, and watching as a growing season develops up and down the roads that cut through our narrow forks of land.

This kind of interconnectivity has helped a new group to flourish, Long Island Sustainable Wine Growing, which, as of early 2015, has 18 members. The group started in 2012 with a manual based on the work of Alice Wise, a researcher at Cornell Cooperative Extension of Suffolk County (remember Cornell from the Finger Lakes?), who has been an instrumental catalyst for good wine. With her co-worker Libby Tarleton, Wise has planted experimental vineyards, worked on enhancing the effectiveness of bird netting, and basically has been the resource for growers when they are stumped diagnosing a problem. Is it a new virus? Is it a fungus? Is it human error?

That's only a few of the ways winemaking can go wrong, even before the grapes get picked. But what we're focusing on here is the way it's gone right. The following pages will tell you about the winemakers, the weather, the vintages, and the evolution of what's in your glass. Long Island is a wine region that here's to stay, and the wine coming out of Long Island is world class.

the

PIONEERS

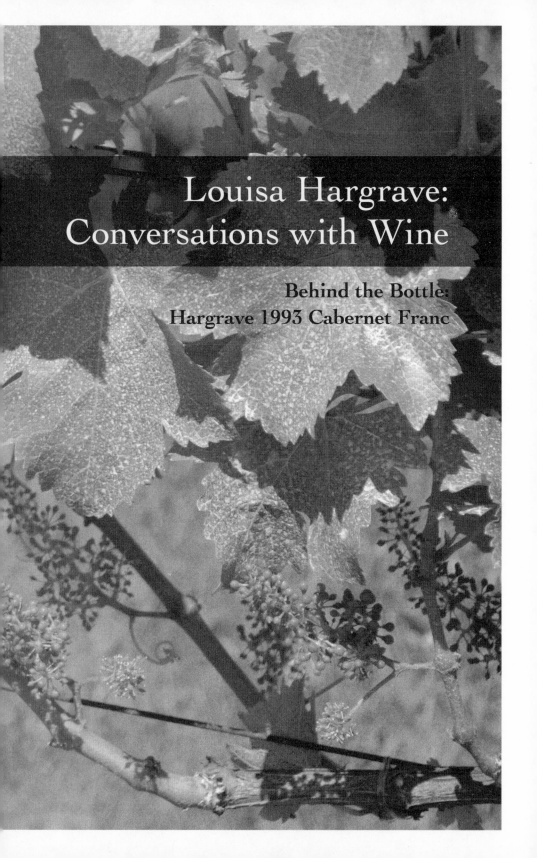

Louisa Hargrave: Conversations with Wine

Behind the Bottle:
Hargrave 1993 Cabernet Franc

"Cabernet franc was supposed to be a blending grape. We didn't even plant any," says Louisa Hargrave, referring to the potato field in Cutchogue she and her former husband, Alex, took over in 1973 to attempt the ill-advised project of starting a vineyard with French wine grapes. Those grapes, Vitis vinifera, include chardonnay and merlot, which produce the best wine. Grapes native to the Americas, such as Vitis riparia or Vitis labrusca, don't really turn into good wine. But the Hargraves were young, had done some research, and were willing to toil in the field. So in went chardonnay, merlot, sauvignon blanc, pinot noir, riesling, and cabernet sauvignon.

Their enthusiasm was infectious, because soon other wide-eyed would-be farmers started clearing land for grape vines and then, at least, they had someone to talk to. The first was Dave Mudd, whose son Steve carries on the family business today. Mudd, an airline pilot who grew up in Kansas and always wanted to be a farmer, had the initial idea of growing grass. But the couple met him at an auction, and he changed his mind. Soon Mudd was the go-to guy to plant your vineyard.

"He had no desire to make wine," says Hargrave. "But he had chunks of time to give. We had a lot of fun; we tried to find out what balanced pruning was by weighing the cuttings." What they wanted to do, she says, was adapt textbook grape growing into something that would work for Long Island. "It was a real friendship and very collegial, which is the way we hoped everything would be."

The next plot Mudd planted was for a real estate developer named Louis Feil, whose business included orange groves in California. "They went big," says Hargrave. "Mudd planted for them chardonnay, merlot, cab franc, cabernet sauvignon, and pinot noir, and they put in electricity for a winery." There was a fight among the partners, says Hargrave, and everything fell apart. "They decided they couldn't afford it and didn't know where they were going, so they asked us if we would come in and take over the vineyard."

The vineyard was a mess, says Hargrave. The Feils had taken the advice of the horticultural department of the Cornell Cooperative Extension up in Geneva and trellised their grapes six feet high. "Crazy for vinifera," says Hargrave. And once she and her husband walked the vineyard, they weren't really sure if the grapes planted were as advertised. "I had to go through the vineyard and figure out which was which" by studying the shape of the leaves, she says. And, as has happened more than once on Long Island—the Lieb family can attest to it—half the chardonnay was really pinot blanc.

"We took it on when the vines were already five or six years old," says Hargrave. "And this vineyard happened to have cabernet franc," obviously a new variety for her. The first winter, she says, they repruned 50 acres, breaking pruning shears at the rate of one per week. By the end, after retraining, she says, the vines were doing quite well. "And when we harvested it, it was delicious!"

The added bonus was a very large crop, eight tons per acre, which is enormous considering today's wineries stick to about three tons per acre max. "We pressed it, put it in barrels for 18 months," she says, "and decided to just make it by itself, no blending with other grapes."

The other bonus, another one of those serendipitous events that has helped many Long Island wineries on the way to success, was the first harvest occurred in 1993, a vintage experienced winemakers still recall with the wistfulness of a very good meal or first love. Even sweeter was that '93 followed on the heels of 1992, a disaster vintage affected by a Filipino volcano whose eruption disrupted agriculture worldwide for a good year.

"That's the one wine that comes to mind as a milestone," says Hargrave. "I was over the moon about it. I think this wine is interesting, because of the fact that we were able to make it. More people were coming out, more people were investing, Mudd was consulting, and he learned by his mistakes, and so did we."

Hargrave's cellar holds a few remaining bottles of the 1993 Cab Franc. She has found them to be uneven, but as she has opened them over the years, it's been emotional. "That's why you make wine in the first place," she says. "In the beginning it was supple and spicy, and it wasn't green. Over the years it still has great fruit, nuance, great oak and acidity." To taste its evolution, she says, "is like meeting another really interesting person that you just want to have another conversation with, because you just don't know what they're going to say. It's a really exciting wine; there's still life in the old boy."

Anyone wanting to know about the birth of Long Island Wine Country would do well to read Hargrave's book *The*

Vineyard, which details the first years of planting, the search for support, and the trials of not just making wine but selling it. But these days Hargrave is more interested in the future. Any conservation about what's coming for local wine includes education for producers and consumers, more inclusion in the New York Wine and Grape Foundation, and promising varieties on the rise.

"I think there's a resurgence now, and I think it's really deserving, but we have to distinguish ourselves from the wines upstate," she says. "I really love Long Island petit verdot. I never would have thought to plant that. But it shows we're different."

Maybe being the matriarch of Long Island wine, as well as no longer having wines to sell, has made Hargrave more clear about what she thinks must be changed and more vocal about how to do it. But lately, she is not shy speaking her mind about the politics of wine promotion in New York State.

"There's nothing about the wines of the Fingers Lakes that's like Long Island wines, and yet we're grouped together," she says. "It is political, but it's worth discussion. It has a place because of statewide funding. It's a sticking point because it does hinder what we can do and how we can market ourselves."

Hargrave brings up the wine research program at Cornell Cooperative Extension of Suffolk County, based in Riverhead, N.Y. Part of the land grant university, the extension often is on the receiving end of state money. Alice Wise, who has been tending a research vineyard there for more than a decade focusing on wines that grow best on Long Island, used to be able to hold annual tastings of her research wines, says Hargrave, and Cornell put the kibosh on that a few years ago. "She had planted interesting grapes," she adds. "We should be able to taste the wines she made."

Hargrave's frustration extends to the media. "I was listening to the New York City NPR station," she says. "And one of the morning talk programs was about a report from Cornell regarding all the winter damage in the Finger Lakes. That has nothing to do with what's going on down here. … Almost everybody out here is making really good wine. Almost better than most California wine. But people have to be ready to like it."

Hargrave sighs. "It's an uphill battle, it really is," she says. "There are people who do really well. But we need to bring in some new faces and some new money, and it could really get exciting."

Richard Olsen-Harbich:
From the Beginning
to the Now

Behind the Bottle:
Bedell Cellars 2010 Taste Red

P lant science. Who goes to school for plant science? In my hometown, people studied finance with the goal of working on Wall Street. Sure it was the suburbs, but so is New Hyde Park, a village in Nassau County 20 miles from New York City where Richard Olsen-Harbich, winemaker at Bedell Cellars since 2010, grew up. Plant science, it seems, is a gateway to a career in wine.

"I finished school at Cornell in 1983," says Olsen-Harbich of the current East Coast equivalent of UC Davis, where career-minded wine students gather in Ithaca, N.Y., on the edge of Cayuga, the central lake in Finger Lakes wine country. "There weren't any majors in viticulture."

But the seed had been planted. His mother, who grew up in Germany, met his father in Manhattan, and the two moved to the Sudetenland, which today is the Czech Republic, to work in the family hotel. There, one of his father's jobs was to fill barrels with wine his grandfather brought back from Moravia. "It's a little bit in my blood," says Olsen-Harbich. Plus, he adds, he's always been interested in how thing grow.

His time in the Finger Lakes put him in touch with Hermann Wiemer, the German wine pioneer who was one of the first to plant riesling in upstate York in 1976. "I fell in love with the creative aspect and the romantic and historical aspect," says Olsen-Harbich. "No other agriculture sector has so much history and is really looked at as intellectually as wine is. That's why I'm still doing it."

Lucky he was, because during his breaks from school he was able to come home and work in the opening years and vineyards of Long Island, which by that time already had a decade of history behind them. His parents had bought a house in Greenport in 1980, and soon he was riding tractors and pruning vines with the father-and-son team of Dave and Steve Mudd. Dave Mudd, an airline pilot, who always really wanted to be a farmer, jumped into vineyard management in 1974, the year after Alex and Louisa Hargrave planted the first European wine grapes on Long Island on their farm in Cutchogue (today, Castello di Borghese). By the mid-'80s the Mudds had their hands in the dirt of nearly every new winegrowing venture on the East End: Bedell, Pindar, Paumanok, Palmer, Peconic Bay Vineyards, Pugliese, and Wölffer Estate.

"I got into the industry as an art form and a craft without really knowing what was going on out here, on the East End," says Olsen-Harbich. It was evident soon enough; by the end of his time with the Mudds, he had helped plant more than 100 acres of vines, installed trellising, and worked as part of the grounds crew. One project was the North Fork Winery, which is now known as Jamesport Vineyards. "I got in at a truly grass-roots level," he says. "I think starting on the ag side, which initially I was more interested in, was what I needed to understand first in terms of my profession."

But professions rarely evolve organically. A catalyst must bomb its way into still waters and provide the activation energy needed to create something new. For Olsen-Harbich that was Lyle Greenfield.

"Lyle was a madman," says Olsen-Harbich. "A brilliant ad guy from the creative side on Madison Avenue and an ex-hippie.

He had a beach house on the South Fork and on a whim bought 74 acres of land in Bridgehampton to plant a vineyard."

Greenfield was all in. He entered into a consulting contract with Wiemer and set out to make the best chardonnay west of Burgundy and east of California.

It would never turn out that way. But Greenfield was able to teach every aspiring winegrower following him what not to do: Do not plant your vineyard in a low-lying area where fog rests and overnight dew doesn't evaporate. Don't put vines where they'll have constantly have wet feet, because they're bordering the wetlands, the ecosystem so characteristic of the coastline of the East End, but which also helps keep the region warm enough to grow grapes. In other words, site selection is important when deciding where to plant grape vines: a lesson local winegrowers still talk about and have taken to the center of their hearts.

But that doesn't mean Greenfield didn't give it the college try. He hired Olsen-Harbich to manage the vineyard, and the two spent 10 years trying to live the dream. At first, the wine was made at Wiemer, in the Finger Lakes, until Greenfield built a winery in the iconic low-slung potato barn on the Bridgehampton-Sag Harbor Turnpike, which now houses the South Fork Natural History Museum & Nature Center.

"I'd spend part of the day wrestling vines that had fallen over in the soggy soil," says Olsen-Harbich, "and then take a shower and try to sell the wine in New York City." At which he had some success, with placements at the 21 Club and the Quilted Giraffe—the restaurant that invented caviar beggar's purses—one owner of which, Susan Wine, eventually opened two retail shops in Manhattan dedicated to New York wine. Her venture, Vintage New York, along with a winery, Rivendell, in the Hudson River Valley, which she started with partner Robert Ransom, both fell to the Great Recession by the beginning of 2009.

The scrappy nature of Bridgehampton Winery was not by design. Olsen-Harbich was working with what he had, which wasn't much. At this stage of the wine business on Long Island, who really knew what you needed? No one had written the manual yet.

"In 1983, I was working a dual harvest," he says, part time in Weimer's vineyard and the rest in Bridgehampton. "I made my first wine, a wild ferment pinot noir, which ended up being a rosé."

Let's pause for a minute and consider the wild ferment. Realizing that wine, among so many other things, is subject to fashion and fads, "wild ferment" has been having a heyday. To turn grape juice into alcohol, yeast is needed. Yeast's job is to eat the sugar in the grape juice, or "must" as the professionals call it, and turn it into alcohol and CO_2. The majority of wineries around the world add commercial yeast to the must. It's reliable and designed to work in a range of temperatures. But yeast is an ambient organism. It lives on the skins of grapes and can be captured in flour to create sour dough bread. That's living dangerously. A fermentation that relies on ambient yeast is risky.

But Olsen-Harbich wasn't able to take that risk into consideration. His "wild ferment" pinot noir happened because he "didn't have any yeast. The winery wasn't set up, and I didn't have any water."

Obstacles to be sure, but that year he was also able to put out a riesling-gewürztraminer blend, a stainless-steel chardonnay, and a rosé.

"At the time I thought they were good," he says, mostly because of what was on offer in the marketplace. All the chardonnays from California were spending time in oak barrels instead of steel and were going through a secondary fermentation that adds a buttery richness to the wine. What he and Greenfield were doing was new! It was exciting!

And it was unsustainable. Because, as the duo soon reluctantly realized, they had planted in the wrong place.

But Olsen-Harbich was philosophical. "Everything is changing constantly," he says. "In order to move forward, and leave this life with something to be proud of, we have to educate ourselves."

The following year, the winery had to purchase a lot of fruit to keep production going. Winter damage followed, which set them back about two years. Then in 1985 Hurricane Gloria hit hard. They were able to produce wine for themselves and the other vineyards without wineries. But the following year, a freeze early in the growing season resulted in 100-percent bud kill. When that happened again, "it was a fatal blow," says Olsen-Harbich. "We left the vineyard, which was in the bottom of a bowl of cold air."

But this didn't elide past accomplishment. The winery was able to get the attention of some opinion makers.

"Bridgehampton Winery was an expensive lesson," says Olsen-Harbich. "But our 1988 Grand Vineyard Selection Chardonnay got 91 points from *Wine Spectator*." This led him to believe they were on to something.

"Hermann Weimer was a leader pushing for vinifera [European vine varieties] as a way for success," says Olsen-Harbich. "But at this time Long Island was kind of an oasis. We could grow red grapes to ripeness. We were seeing this area just explode; no one had thought we could grow these kind of grapes in New York."

To Olsen-Harbich's mind, grapes are meant to be planted on the East End. "We have 210 growing-season days," he says; the average grape vine needs at minimum 100 days to get ripe. "We're in the warmest part of New York State," as recorded by the degree-day standard of scientists employed by Cornell Cooperative Extension, the authority on optimum plant conditions on Long Island.

Aside from the importance of site selection, Olsen-Harbich says he learned what Long Island was capable of: making its own distinct style of wine, wine that was nothing like the produce of the warm and consistent vintages of California.

But consumers hadn't figured it out yet. "We were compared to the West Coast, so people thought the wines fell short instead of appreciating them for they were: elegant, with natural acidity; the kind of wines that made Bordeaux and Burgundy famous," he says. "That took a long time for us to figure out and for writers to figure out. Thankfully it was, and that's where we are today."

In 1993 Bridgehampton sold to Lenz, and Olsen-Harbich left for a two-year stint as the general manager of Hargrave Vineyards. After that, he started a consulting agency, Wine Works, with Larry Perrine, a soil scientist who was creating his own impact on the industry. The two helped Schneider, Peconic Bay Winery, Raphael, Channing Daughters, and Martha Clara get their businesses going. The partnership ended when Olsen-Harbich became the winemaker at Raphael in 1996, and Perrine went to Channing.

Raphael's initial focus was on merlot. For help with this, the winery took on Paul Pontallier, the wine director at the famous left-bank Bordeaux Chateau Margeaux. Pontallier had been to Long Island before; in February 1988 the wineries organized a two-day symposium that brought Bordeaux producers to walk the vineyards and visit the wineries. Both regions work within a maritime climate, and Long Island producers believed they could learn a lot from the people of a region that had been making wine for centuries.

"I think that was a real turning point," says Olsen-Harbich, "a dividing line between the early days and when the region started hitting its stride. It made us think about where we wanted to end up, because, ultimately we have more in common with Bordeaux, with its climate and four full seasons each year. We were inspired."

Like Bordeaux, Long Island has to grow in conditions that are less than perfect, says Olsen-Harbich. "The best wines in the world are grown in regions that aren't perfect. It makes it that much more of a triumph for us."

Pontallier worked with Raphael for nine years. "It was an important guiding force for me," says Olsen-Harbich. "I learned from him to use feel and the senses rather than just technology, to pay attention to what the vineyard is doing, to look at it holistically and go with what the vineyard's giving you. Don't try to direct it as much as embrace it."

While at Raphael, Olsen-Harbich helped start the Long Island Merlot Alliance and secure grants to study the flavor and aroma profiles of the merlot grape. He also initiated the establishment of the American Viticultural Area of Long Island: The Hamptons, North Fork of Long Island, and Long Island. To put these names on a label, 85 percent of a wine's fruit must come from that region. Similar systems have been in place in Europe for centuries to prevent wine fraud and protect place names.

In 2010 Olsen-Harbich went to Bedell, where he serves as head winemaker of one of the region's most modern wineries in terms of production and marketing. The change has freed him to be more creative, he says, and to learn more about how grapes grow in the varied soil of Long Island.

"In one area of the vineyard it can be solid gray clay beneath the topsoil," he says. "And a few feet away it's sand just like you find on the beach." These conditions figure significantly in the choices he makes when picking, planting, vinifying, and blending. An example of this is Bedell's 2010 Taste Red, a wine Olsen-Harbich choose because it represents what he feels Long Island is capable of, taking in all the possibilities our soils, climate, and grapes present a winemaker.

Taste Red is also evidence of Long Island's ability to make red wine, which distinguishes it from other wine-producing regions in the Northeast.

The 2010 vintage gave Olsen-Harbich the opportunity to showcase all of the above. The weather was beautiful, dry and hot, which gives vineyard managers the all-important element of choice when picking. Olsen-Harbich took advantage of this to co-ferment grapes because he could pick them at the same time.

For the Taste Red, the blend was 60 percent merlot, 20 percent syrah, 12 percent petit verdot, 6 percent cabernet franc, and 2 percent malbec. To enhance the aromatics, Olsen-Harbich threw in some chardonnay grapes during fermentation. To make the wine more complex, he saved the skins from the petit verdot after they were drawn off and put them back into the blend as it fermented.

"What happens when it co-ferments," he says, "is that it gives the wine its own aromatic signature. Making this wine was like throwing paint on a canvas and not really following a recipe. More like Jackson Pollack, less like DaVinci." This seemingly haphazard method also used ambient yeast. And unlike his days at Bridgehampton, he did it on purpose.

The heightened aromatics Long Island is capable of, says Olsen-Harbich, should be celebrated. "It's not like the over-ripe character of West Coast wines. This is something the Old World has done for years."

It's a theme Olsen-Harbich returns to again and again: how Long Island is able to create wines like nowhere else in the world, and to get out from under the anxiety of influence all we have to do is listen to the grapes.

"There's a style that's been evolving in the wines I make," he says, "where I've come to in the last 10 years. There's more homeostasis, less intervention and a balance. There's a lot of possible changes you can make to a wine, a lot of things you can influence, but I've learned to kind of just let it be what it is."

Olsen-Harbich credits Pontallier with this perspective, even though he has now gone his own way.

"It's probably similar to a writer finding her own voice, or mimicking the style of someone you like; it's what a lot of artists do," he says. "I think we were like that as a region. But now we're more confident in what we are able to grow."

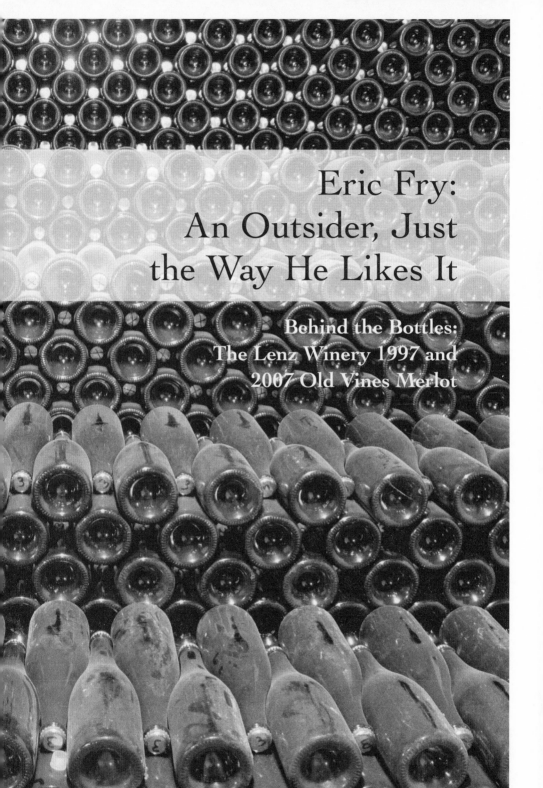

Eric Fry:
An Outsider, Just
the Way He Likes It

Behind the Bottles:
The Lenz Winery 1997 and
2007 Old Vines Merlot

A 28-year veteran of Long Island Wine Country, Lenz winemaker Eric Fry has a reputation as an iconoclast, a rebel, an outsider who does things his own way. The rest of you be damned. He considers terroir a marketing concept dreamed up by the French. He calls biodynamics voodoo. He waits longer than anyone to release his wines and refuses to give out his cell phone number, because he doesn't want to waste time talking on the phone. The winery, in a renovated barn—a long-ago-renovated barn—still only has one phone line, which receives both calls and faxes. His office is like installation art, if installation art were the result of nearly 30 years of use by an absent-minded professor. Few have seen him clean-shaven or dressed in anything other than denim overalls. His once-red beard is now streaked with gray, as is his ponytail. You're not going to see him in full color on the cover of a brochure. And the Lenz Winery is the only one to have consistently refused to join the Long Island Wine Council.

But that's not the whole story. Talk to any winemaker, and they'll tell you about the things they learned from Fry and his comrade in arms, vineyard manager Sam McCullough, who started working at Lenz in 1989, the year after Fry started. Fry was the first to let his grapes hang longer than anyone else's. "In the beginning everyone made fun me, 'Oh, we're all done harvesting, so now Eric will start picking,'" he says. "Then a few years later it became a competition, to see who could pick the latest, because they saw it worked."

Fry also has regularly organized winemaker dinners—no press allowed!—so everyone could get together and taste what the others were up to. In the early years, the dinners were held at Ross's North Fork, the Southold restaurant started by John Ross in 1974 that is universally acknowledged as the cradle of the local food movement on the East End. Fry wanted to avoid "cellar palate," which can happen when the only wine you taste is your own. Attendees are also encouraged to bring wine from other regions to expand their palates.

But these are not things Fry readily advertises. He describes himself as an "iconoclast" going all the way back to the high school of his 5,000-person basketball crazy hometown in Indiana. The school's gym, he says, could seat the entire town. "And I hated basketball."

But the town was surrounded by farms growing corn and beans and pigs. Fry found his summer jobs there, baling hay, and many of his relatives lived way outside of town working their own farms.

Fry went to school at the University of Indiana and studied microbiology and phycology. "I might be messing with you right now," he winks. He started with math, but found it horribly boring; he switched to chemistry and then ran into a really good microbiology teacher. "The difference between chemistry and microbiology is life," he says. "One is alive, the other isn't."

Upon graduation, he and his girlfriend promptly moved to California, "where our political views were more acceptable," and landed with some friends in Napa.

"I needed a job," he says. So he checked out some wineries and then walked into Mondavi and told them he had a degree in microbiology. "They grabbed me on the spot," he says, "just because they had recently decided they needed a microbiologist. It was nuts."

It was also 1976, the same year a California chardonnay took top honors at the blind tasting that came to be known as the Judgment of Paris. California wine was taking off.

Fry was tasked with clearing the winery of brettanomyces, a strain of yeast that affects the taste and smell of wine. He hates brett to this day. "You'll never find it here," he says. And he loved his time at Mondavi. They sent him to UC Davis to take classes and included him in their weekly meeting; even though he was the new guy, he got to sit at the table. "They were great people," says Fry. "Robert taught me things that still resonate today. He was an impressive guy; he had charisma, the kind where everyone turned their head when he walked into a room. That kind of charisma."

Fry also feels lucky to have worked with Zelma Long, Mondavi's winemaker at the time. Long, the second woman to enroll in the master's in oenology program at Davis, is still in the business with a winery in South Africa and one in Napa Valley. "Looking back at it," he says, "the luck was incredible. I went to the University of Mondavi. I learned about wine there. I can't think of a better place to start."

But Fry got tired of the lab; at Mondavi, he says, there was no blurring of the lines between the lab and the cellar. He took off for Europe, and returned to apply for jobs as an assistant winemaker. He was hired at Jordan, where he split his time between the lab and the cellar.

There his lucky streak continued; he fell under the tutelage of André Tchelistcheff, one of the most heralded winemakers in California, who was consulting at Jordan. "He was 85 years old," says Fry, but not too old to drag race. "He had a 260Z and I had a 280Z, and we would race through Knights Valley on the way to work. I was a stupid young kid. But he was 85! He was sort of like a god, a very nice guy."

But Fry knew it would be a long time before he would be able to head his own cellar in Napa Valley. "I wanted to be a winemaker," he says, "be in control and make my own wines." Tchelistcheff recognized this and told Fry about an old friend of his in the Finger Lakes who was looking for a winemaker. "He told me I could be a big fish in a small pond," says Fry. "And he was right. There was so much competition in Napa."

So in 1985 Fry ended up at the door of Dr. Konstantin Frank's Vinifera Wine Cellars in Hammondsport. "I looked at the place," he says, "and thought 'I could make good wine here.'" Fry had lucked into another great position. In 1962 Frank was the first to plant vinifera, or European grape vines, in New York. He believed it was the rootstock, not the cold, preventing ripeness. Soon his winery was becoming famous for its riesling, what is now the signature grape of the Finger Lakes. "I was there for four years," says Fry. "And I think made some really nice wines; the reds were more of a challenge."

Then, in 1988 Fry got a call from a guy on Long Island. "He wanted me to help him find a winemaker," Fry said. It was Peter Carroll from Lenz in Peconic, who that year, with a partner, spent $1 million to buy the winery from its founders, Peter and Pat Lenz. The vines onsite had been planted in 1979, and Fry got the vibe. "I liked it down here," he says. "The Finger Lakes can be a little bit dismal and the winters are rough." But the

East End was an hour and a half from New York City, and what Fry tasted in the grapes was positive. "The vineyards needed a little work," he adds. But nothing too tricky. "It was just a matter of getting the vineyards and the winery in sync."

He believes he didn't get there until 1993, a spectacular vintage that turned attention to Long Island wine. "Long Island really didn't come into its own until 1993," says Fry. "In 1990, I didn't have my act together, but somewhere after '91 we all started to work together and solved a lot of problems." Nothing, however, could solve the problem of the 1992 vintage when an eruption of a volcano in the Philippines, Mount Pinatubo, the year before disturbed the weather worldwide by casting ash into the atmosphere.

But '93. "In 1993, that's when we jumped on the world stage," says Fry. "It all came together. Kip [Bedell] would probably say it happened in '91, but I wasn't ready yet."

Since then, Fry has been turning out consistently distinctive wine that few could mistake for another producer. His style is part theory, part art, and no small amount of microbiology. But he's not an ideologue; while he sticks to fairly exacting techniques, he's more than willing to say his wines have evolved over the years, departing from what he calls a Burgundian reductive style to wines with more fruit and less oak. "The public likes it fresher and cleaner," he says.

Fry chose to show this progression by opening a 1997 and a 2007 Old Vines Merlot. "The two merlots are 10 years apart. I hope it will show a little evolution in style," he shrugs. "Mainly what's it's going to show is bottle age.

"I've been on Long Island 25 years now, and what I've tried to do is deepen the structure of the wine," Fry says. "My style is reductive and ripe grapes are the secret. Wait, there is no secret, but if there were it is ripe grapes."

To start, Fry makes wine with a consistent pH—he likes to keep it low to maintain acid—and doesn't mind adjusting the levels to keep it at what he calls "correct pH." He also admits he will pick early, for his whites, to keep a fresh acidity. For the reds his reductive Burgundian style means letting alcoholic fermentation, and the secondary malo-lactic fermentation, take their own sweet time. This prevents excess exposure to oxygen. "It's a matter of being more patient and less fastidious in the beginning. I'll press and rack it [to remove sediment] within 48 hours," he says, "and then put it in barrel a little dirty. The grape particles settle out right away and the yeast is still alive. This not only imparts flavor but the chemicals absorb oxygen. Then it goes through a long slow ML [malo-lactic] that finishes in March." Another way of doing it, which Fry calls the Bordeaux style, is to "press, shove it through ML and then put it in barrel."

Fry admits his style is not for everyone. "To me it is desirable and gives the wines complexity and almost a mushroomy, earthy character. But it's extremely old school. The few people who understood it loved it—and loved it enough for us to sell out—but more people are going to understand wine with a bit more happy fruit." Old age has taught him that, he says. "I lean scientific in my winemaking, but I try to ignore it. Now if science says one thing and my palate says something else, that's what I go with."

Lenz's Old Vines Merlot is made from grapes grown on vines planted in 1979, according to Peter Carroll's records. Visitors can see them in the vineyard just northwest of the tasting room. The thick trunks and the knobby contorted canes are evidence of their age. Older vines produce less fruit than productive youthful ones, so the grapes are more concentrated. These vines have been around so long because their quality year to year indicates they were planted in a good site.

Both the 1997 and the 2007 were made from grapes picked from this plot. Fry used the same technique, the same yeast, and the same kind of French oak barrels, though with probably more new oak in 1997.

In the glass the colors are very similar; the 2007 has more fruit aromas but not much more than the 1997. However, they both have that distinctive Lenz smell: an aroma that almost conveys weight, a richness that mingles with the ripe fruit and mint and chocolate typical of merlot grown in the Pomerol region in France. Fry takes this as a compliment.

He tastes the 1997. "This is 15 years old and still has nice fruit, nice richness and body; it's not tired. I expected it to be much more earthy and mushroomy." He picks up the 2007. "They're actually remarkably similar." The wines are also proof that another of Fry's goals, to make wines that will age, is achievable. The 1997, he says, is "still a lively wine, totally drinkable at age 17. I'm not trying to make pop wine; you want to be able to put a bottle down and age it."

This is also a part of the business plan at Lenz. Long ago they noticed that "as we ran out of the vintage, it was tasting the best we ever tasted," says Fry. "We were releasing too soon." In 2014, Lenz's current vintage of the Old Vines Merlot is the 2007. "We wait as long as it takes," he says. The 2007 was bottled in '09 and lay in bottle for five years. By doing so, the winery is able to charge more money per bottle; age does add value to wine, but storing that many back vintages is expensive. It's easier to sell your wines early to ensure consistent revenue.

Holding wines is not an uncommon practice on Long Island, but everyone else sold out of their 2007 reds a while ago, although some are still sitting in libraries. Old Vines Merlot goes for $60 in the tasting room and sells out to visitors and members of their wine club. "We price it so it doesn't fly out the door," says Fry. "I'm annoyed right now because our bubbly is selling too fast. I want to up the price, so it doesn't sell too quickly." Contriving to get customers to put off buying your product seems kooky, but it's been working for Lenz.

So is Fry's commitment to single-varietal wines. He has made some one-off blends for wine club members, but Fry's not interested. "I've got my varietals, and I'm going to stick to them. I'm not going to start making orange wine."

But he knows others disagree, sometimes vehemently. "It's really funny because I've had upstart winemakers as interns. They're all striving for attention, so they're doing goofy wines," he says. "I'm the old fart just kind of plugging away making what's dependable year in and year out. The young guys don't want to do my style because it's been done. But it's definitive; if you've experienced it for a while, it should stand right out."

He adds, "I like merlot. I like what it tastes like."

Roman Roth: Aging Gracefully

Behind the Bottles: Wölffer Estate 1997 Chardonnay and 2012 White Mischief chardonnay; Grapes of Roth 2008 Merlot; Wölffer Estate 2005 Christian Cuvée merlot blend

To taste wine with Wölffer winemaker Roman Roth, you might want to dress up first. Don't expect a casual affair where he stands behind the tasting bar searching out bottles and wine glasses, or an impromptu sampling in the tank room where you stand up and spit in the drains on the floor. No, Roth will have the bottles already selected and matched with the appropriate glassware. Spittoons will be on the table for each taster, and it will all be set up in the spectacular barrel room in the Wölffer cellar, where a half-circular table is fitted into an alcove the staff calls the Crescent. Roth will have notes on hand and a ready smile for the camera. He will tell some jokes, mostly at his own expense and flat out set himself to the task of showing the longevity of Long Island wine. "I wish I would age as well as my wines," he says with a half wink.

He goes right for Wölffer's 1997 Estate Selection Chardonnay. "I picked this one because it can show how classy and elegant these wines are," he says, adding that he could have shown a '93 or a '94 or a '95, but that would have been too easy. Those vintages are enshrined in Long Island lore because their beautiful hot weather made great wine. Wine that helps spur growth in the industry. No, Roth picked the 1997 because to him, at this time, it still displays "balance with food-friendly acidity dancing on your tongue. It's not flabby or fat. This is a wine with finesse, which is so fashionable now."

The bottle demonstrated, once again, the adage that there's no good wine, only good bottles. From the time it is pressed to the time wine is labeled and boxed—and then drunk—wine is a living thing. This can guarantee that any case is going to have bottle variation. The wine didn't have the fresh fruit aromas Roth had found in another '97 opened earlier in the week.

"This is not the best example," says Roth, "but you can taste our terroir, the way our grapes ripen in the vineyard. You can taste the sun-drenched grape skins; it's not just about alcohol, it's about acidity and fruit."

The wine is a deep gold. "You get orange peel, ripe canta-loupe, and a fine toasty almond note," he says. "And then you get the mouthfeel; it's creamy, leesy with acidity and miner-ality that balances with the toastiness of the oak. And then the alcohol is the thread that weaves it all together. This is classic; it's why chardonnay is such a great variety."

The "leesy" element Roth is talking about comes from leaving newly fermented wine on the lees, or the dead yeast cells, while it ages in barrel. This wine spent eight months with lees contact. It's a signature of his wine and, once used to it, observant wine drinkers detect it right away. But there's a theory behind it.

"If you don't do a long lees contact," says Roth, "it's like ripping a child away from its mother." He reaches out and makes a grabbing motion. "It'll never have the time to bond, to give flavor and expression, to form the wine, to have character. That's why my whites have tannins."

For Roth, chardonnay is a great variety, and Wölffer Estate in Sagaponack on the South Fork, less than two-and-a-half miles from the Atlantic Ocean, is a great place to grow it. "We pick very ripe," he says. "In Burgundy [the French region that produces the most famous, and famously expensive, chardon-nays] you need 100 days, from mid flower to mid maturity. Here we get 120 and one-half days. That's tremendously long hang time. Yet you only get 13.5 percent alcohol. The flavors don't go into the tropical, like banana or pineapple." The long hang time allows Roth and other vineyard managers and wine-makers to take their time picking the fruit. Chardonnay grapes picked just after ripening bring a citrus flavor to the wine. Pick a little later and you get apple. Then the different batches can be blended together for a more complex wine.

Roth arrived in Long Island just in time to experience the disastrous vintage of 1992, the year fallout from the eruption of Mount Pinatubo in the Philippines let very little sunlight reach the vines. He wasn't daunted; he knew a winemaker needs three to four years to see how the winery and the vineyard can work together. Besides, he liked it in the Hamptons. And his new boss was also German and a Pisces.

Roth was born in Rottweil, Germany, kind of in its south-west corner, where his father was a winemaker and a cooper, the professional that makes wine barrels. "I grew up with lots of wine around me," he says, "and a lot of passion and appreciation." His father traveled north to work in the riesling-dominated Rheingau and eventually settled down as a wine merchant. But he also was a home distiller and made cider. Roth's brother, 10 years his senior, took over the business, and in 1982 Roth started an apprenticeship at the Kaiserstuhl Wine Cooperative in Oberrotweil, Germany, that had a three-year program with one month spent in school and the next two in the field.

In 1986 he traveled to California to see how they did it in the New World. How he did it was by working at Saintsbury and finding an Australian wife, Dushy, while on a tour of Universal Studios in Los Angeles. Roth had to return to Germany to do the mandatory military service, which was followed by a quick trip to Australia, where he worked at Rosemount Estate. "That was very inspiring," he says. "I learned the whole wine language there, of how to discuss it. Before that, all I could offer was 'This is good.'"

The couple moved to back Germany, and Roth became a winemaker at Winzerkeller Wiesloch near Heidelberg. While there he earned a master's degree in winemaking and a cellar master degree from the College for Oenology and Viticulture in Weinsberg.

Before long he started to look around for more opportunity. He scanned websites and came across something about a winery on Long Island. "I had to go to the library and look it up," he says, "and I found one entry saying the Hargraves had planned a vineyard in 1973. There was certainly not a lot written about Long Island." But it wouldn't be like going into the middle of the outback, like he was at Rosemount, where there was a video store and a pub and that's it. "New York was a five-dollar bus ride away," he says. "It was the Hamptons. How bad could it be?"

Soon after, Roth and his wife had their first meeting with Christian Wölffer, the successful cosmopolitan international bon vivant who wanted to turn a big piece of property in a very desirable area into a winery and a horse farm. "Christian flew to Germany to meet me and Dushy," says Roth. "It was a beautiful Sunday morning in May in 1992, and we were to meet at 8 a.m. I brought along a bottle of the wine—a barrel-fermented pinot blanc—I had made for our wedding. We drove out in my mother's big BMW and ended up in a big, amazing garden in a small town next to the Stuttgart airport, just a big tree, three glasses and a corkscrew."

Wölffer said he wanted someone young, and Roth believed their creative energies were in sync. "He told me I could buy whatever I wanted for the winery to just make the best wine possible."

At 26 years old, Roth packed up his three bags and his guitar and moved, arriving with his wife in the Hamptons in August 1992.

Wölffer, who had started planting his vineyard in 1987, was in the middle of planning a winery/tasting room that would introduce a new aesthetic to wine country. No thank you renovated potato barn; Wölffer followed the example of Tuscany, with ochre-hued stucco walls and large beams lining cathedral ceilings. Stained glass doors were designed to open to an elevated patio with a 180-degree view of the vineyard.

But that wasn't there for Roth's first vintage. He was working in a metal building and the 1991 was made at Peconic Bay Winery and Bridgehampton Winery. Mount Pinatubo was responsible for 13 rainy weekends. "It was the worst vintage in the Hamptons," says Roth. "But, even in that tricky year, we made a nice chardonnay from vines that had been planted in 1988."

Roth has now been the only winemaker in the past 22 years to operate the presses, decide how long to leave a wine in oak, and walk the vineyards and tank rooms at Wölffer Estate. Vineyard managers have come and gone—there's the story of one guy, known as the Woodchuck, who took a swing at Roth with a crow bar—but the current manager, Richard Pisacano, has been there since 1997. He also owns his own vineyard; his grapes are turned into wine at Wölffer with Roth's help.

Like everyone who survived the vintage of 1992, Roth was rewarded with a string of great vintages. "The '93 was amazing," says Roth, "fantastic. Then the '94 for chardonnay was a dream, and then the fantastic '95. Our wines were in all the New York Times four-star restaurants: La Caravelle, Le Bernardin, Daniel, Chanterelle and Lespinasse."

Roth was sold on the region's potential. "We saw we could make wines to stand up to the great Burgundies." In 1993, the East End greeted winemakers from California, France, and Australia for a chardonnay symposium. "People were very impressed with the region's wines," he says.

That's when Wölffer got excited, says Roth. Previously the winery had been called Sag Pond Vineyard. Now Wölffer wanted his name on the label; by 1995 the first spade went into the ground to build the winery and by 1997 it opened. Wölffer kept planting grapes and now the 175-acre estate has 55 acres under vine. "In the early days," says Roth, "Wölffer had amazing success with the chardonnays. It's the reason we are Wölffer today."

But, like any creative type, Roth is not one to rest on laurels. He now makes three chardonnays with three combinations of techniques and three different price points. The entry-level chardonnay retails for $19; it uses minimal oak and stays on the lees for four and a half months. The middle chardonnay is called Perle after one of Christian Wölffer's horses and is made from select handpicked grapes. The wine spends more time in new oak and in oak overall. It stays on the lees for eight and a half months and sells for $30.

To contrast with the 1997 chardonnay he had opened earlier, Roth chose the 2012 White Mischief, the winery's top-of-the-line chardonnay made from 100-percent Dijon clones planted in 1993. 2012 was tricky because of the hit the region took from Superstorm Sandy in late October. Thanks to a warm spring and summer, wineries were able to harvest before the storm. For White Mischief, also named after one of Wölffer's horses, the grapes were harvested by hand and only free-run juice went into the fermenters; no juice pressed from the skins, stems, and seeds was added. The wine was exposed to 25-percent new oak, which imparts the most flavor, and it spent seven and a half months on the mother lees.

"We worked so clean the way we handpicked this wine," says Roth. "In this fruit there was not a rotten berry. If you have that, your juice settles so much nicer, and I can work with a more traditional method." Every effort was made to minimize exposure to oxygen. "When we top off [the barrels from which aging wine has evaporated], we immerse the spout. Why add oxygen? You can force it up the curve, or you can protect it and 20, 30 years of aging will do that."

Roth swirls and then sips the wine. "There's an oiliness about this wine," he says. "The ambient yeast gives it more glycerin. There are fresh flavors, but there's a lushness that comes along. Then the barrel fermentation gives it structure and a classic finish. There's this tension, this freshness and slow and steady, painfully slow, fermentation that gives it a focus, a vibrancy."

He pauses, "I think that's why it's so popular; it's great fresh vibrant wine that's just screaming for food."

For Roth, the site's 120-day hang time makes possible a flavor profile that is still crisp and fresh due to the cool breeze from the ocean, conditions not far off from France's Bordeaux, which translates to "the edge of the water."

"Bordeaux would make wonderful chardonnay," says Roth, "but they're not allowed to grow it." (Roth is not the only winemaker grateful European wine laws do not apply to Long Island.) He's also pleased with the way the vines have aged. "They have a much healthier pH," he says, "so the grapes are more balanced when they come in." He adds, "In the past we were forced to pick earlier, because the pH would go so high, and you'd make this soapy wine that wasn't stable, and the fermentation was not as healthy. The age of the vines helps with that.

"We have a focus on great chardonnay," says Roth, "and I'm proud of all the wines. I don't have a dog in the house. But we are in a tourist area and have to have different varieties.

I believe merlot, cabernet franc, sauvignon blanc, and trebbiano all do very well here."

No fooling around, Roth has had some success with merlot. Serendipitously, the first two bottlings of his private label—which he makes at Wölffer from purchased North Fork grapes—the 2001 and 2002 Grapes of Roth Merlot were released by 2006, the same year David Schildknecht, a reviewer from the *Wine Advocate,* visited Long Island. The wines were awarded a 91 and a 92, respectively.

"I wanted to make something unique, that would stand up to the best in the world," he says. "I only make 225 cases of it, so you really work it, massage every berry." For our tasting Roth opened a bottle of his 2008 Grapes of Roth Merlot. "It was not one of our great years," he says, "and that's why I'm so proud of it."

Like Eric Fry of the Lenz Winery, whom we will meet later, Roth hews to a traditional style, one he describes as rustic. "But you want to have an intensity that soars above the rustic character, something that cuts through the fat of the duck," he says. For Grapes of Roth Merlot, Roth aims for a wine that's not just red, fruity, and alcoholic but is about the layers and the textures in between those structural elements. To do so, again like Fry, the wine goes through the secondary fermentation that changes malic acid to lactic acid in a barrel, instead of a stainless steel tank, over the course of five to six months. "It makes it much tighter, much denser," says Roth. The 2008 spent 21 months in oak barrels with 40-percent new oak and is his current vintage. Roth only makes this wine in good vintage years and holds them until he feels they're ready to be released. For example, he released his 2007 before the 2006, because he felt the 2006 needed more time.

Today, he believes the 2008 is still a baby but is already getting what he calls the "tertiary" flavors wines develop after some time in bottle. It's when the fresh fruit flavors and aromas evolve to earthy dried fruit. Roth smells the wine. "It's pure," he says. "It's not this sweet fruit; the alcohol isn't coming out; you get olive flavors, cassis, and toasted oak. But it doesn't give you everything in the first sniff. The wine will change as you drink it." His method allowed very little oxygen to interfere during vinification and aging. "I keep it clean," he says. "That's why when you smell leather, you smell Hermes leather, not some cheap leather." Roth smiles and takes a sip. "There's a subtle power, layers of texture. It's not a tannic monster. And a little bit of acidity, which is what makes Italian reds so nice. The lots of time on the lees gives you this tight mossy texture; it's not your tootie-fruitie merlot. This has nothing to do with California merlot." The wine retails for $100, and Roth is able to sell all of it but laments a comparison imbalance. "This is my top of the line, but people compare it to a $400 top of the line California wine. That's just the way it is."

The last bottle Roth opens is the 2005 Christian's Cuvée, a merlot made from Wölffer fruit. He pours it from a 375-milliliter bottle, which he uses to assess readiness for release because smaller bottles mature faster. "This is how great Long Island can be," he says. "Our wines can stand up to the best in the world." The grapes for this merlot were planted in 1990 and were first bottled as Christian's Cuvée in 2000. Like the Grapes of Roth, he doesn't make it every year, and it's normally 100-percent merlot. "It's such a linear wine," he says. "It's not like a football player; it's all about the minerality." I consider asking him if he means an American football player or a soccer player but realize it probably wouldn't clarify his statement.

The 2005 vintage has its own famous back story. The summer growing season was so hot and dry that "Vintage of the Century" was starting to form on people's lips. By Columbus Day weekend in mid-October, no one could form any words because they were gaping at the 17 inches of rain that fell over eight days, flooding vineyards and turning pristine dry grapes into soggy rot-magnets. If the grapes didn't rot, they split because the vines drew up too much water too quickly.

"We lost 15 percent to split," says Roth, "and 30 percent to dehydration. It was such a crazy freak occurrence." But still he loves the wine. "The Grapes of Roth is bigger than the Christian's Cuvée, but it's not as balanced. It has intensity and power and this classic structure." Roth believes the difference between the two is definitely a result of the origin of the grapes. "North Fork grapes have more alcohol," he says. "And the ripening curve is different. It stays cooler at night longer down here. It makes for a more elegant wine. You can take your time with this wine, mainly because it doesn't overload you and stuff you."

the
CRAFTSMEN

Russell Hearn:
An Aussie in New York

Behind the Bottles: Pellegrini Vineyards
1994 and 1995 Encore, a red blend

Russell Hearn conducts interviews with a calculator handy. Questions are answered after calculations are made and checked again. In his house, the reality that wine is a business is never far behind the artistry and science needed to produce quality. No matter how good your wine is, if you can't sell it, it's just a lot of really good juice taking up space in a warehouse. Evidence of Hearn's business acumen is Premium Wine Group, which at the time of its opening was the only winery-for-hire, or custom crush facility, east of the Mississippi. Premium was a great idea. There were so many people wanting to make wine on Long Island who didn't have the capital to buy presses, de-stemmers, tanks, barrels, and bottling lines. Some of his customers—he started with eight in 2000—had their own vineyards but no winery. Others were establishing a brand with purchased grapes but had no winery either.

Today, Premium has 26 customers, the facilities to make 100,000 cases per year, and state-of-the-art bottling lines for sparkling wines, screw caps, and wine in a bag/box. The calculator comes out. "We were bottling 25,000 cases in the first year," says Hearn. "In 2001, we had a full-time staff of four. Now we employ nine people full time and two people part time, with three or four brought in for harvest." Premium has 138 tanks capable of processing 250,000 gallons of wine, and in 2014 the 23,000-square-foot space is the subject of blueprints outlining expansion plans to enlarge storage and barrel rooms and add more offices. The tiny tasting room in the front, which previously only sold wine from Lieb Cellars— Mark Lieb was an original investor in Premium—reopened in

May 2014 as the Tasting Group, a collaborative tasting room selling wine from Premium's customers and Hearn's own brands, Suhru and T'Jara.

"It's been very successful," says Hearn. "Sparkling Pointe started here. And after 14 years, Martha Clara is still here. I would have been happy with five customers. I think the Long Island wine landscape would be dramatically different today if it didn't have Premium. We wouldn't have all these boutique producers."

Russell Hearn was born in Singapore—on Australian soil—to a father serving in the Air Force. But he was raised in Perth, where the family returned when he was young. His mother was in the wine industry, working in marketing for Sandleford, the second oldest winery in Western Australia, which now has vineyards in the Margaret River region and the Swan Valley. "There were 30 wineries then," says Hearn, "including the place I started, Houghton Wines. They were making 800,000 cases when I was there. Now they're making a million and a quarter."

During summers, Hearn found work at the local wineries, and in 1979 started a five-year tenure at Houghton's with an apprenticeship. In the meantime he went to a technical school to study chemistry.

The wine business in Western Australia was going gangbusters at that time, drawing on a long history. Houghton's first vintage was in 1852; Western Australia was only settled in 1829. By the time Hearn started working, Australian wineries started aggressively going after the export market. "In 1979," says Hearn, "Houghton made a varietal chardonnay for the first time. Their main wine was Classic White, a blend. Then, they had only 80 acres of chardonnay planted. At the time that was something like 70 percent of all the chardonnay in Australia. Now there are probably eight million cases of chardonnay produced in Australia."

Hearn notes the growth in exports gave Australian wine a head start over wine produced in the United States. The years of Prohibition, from 1920 to 1933, set American wine way behind the rest of the world. So when tastes in the U.S. turned from liquor to wine in the 1970s, the Australians were there with experience and product. In 1979, Houghton was bought by the conglomerate Hardys, a wine producer in business since 1850. "We were producing less than 10 million cases in the seventies," says Hearn. "By the nineties, it was 20 million. I got in at a good time."

Without an interruption in production, like Prohibition in the U.S., Australian wineries were able to band together and form a self-regulating authority that not only protected the Australian brand but funded research and concentrated marketing power. "The information was nationwide," says Hearn. "A small appellation in the Swan Valley had access to the same data as producers in the Yarra Valley."

After his time at Houghton, Hearn took the wine student tour, participating in exchanges in Burgundy in the tiny appellation of Aloxe-Corton with Domaine Maurice Chapuis. "That was an eye-opening experience," says Hearn. He went to New Zealand, where in 1973 growers in the region of Marlborough had planted the first sauvignon blanc vines—the same year the Hargraves first planted European grape vines on Long Island—a wine (think Cloudy Bay) that would soon take the world by storm.

Hardys was eventually sold to Constellation, a reigning conglomerate, but Hearn had already found his destiny in New Zealand in the form of an American girl who was backpacking with a friend. "Now it's 29 years and counting," says Hearn. His wife Sue was from Massachusetts; he visited and got a job at Commonwealth Winery in Plymouth. "I worked there for four years and then we moved to Virginia." The couple spent 1988 and 1989 trying to make a career in the Old Dominion state, but it didn't work. "We really didn't fit there," says Hearn. But he was able to come to Long Island in 1988 for the maritime climate winegrowing symposium that included producers from Bordeaux and some local talent.

At that point the choice became obvious. Either move back to Australia or stay on the East Coast. "California is a warm climate; if we were going to move there, we might as well have moved to Australia," says Hearn. Long Island it was. Hearn spent 1990 and 1992 consulting with Paumanok and Standing Stone, a winery in the Finger Lakes. But fate visited in 1991, when Hearn met Bob Pellegrini, a very successful designer of annual corporate reports, who wanted to take his passion for wine to the level of vineyard ownership.

Hearn was hooked. He loved the climate and potential of the North Fork, which he believed had more potential as a growing region than the South Fork. "The North Fork is definitely warmer," says Hearn. "And more affected by shallower bodies of water" that don't hold the cold like the Atlantic Ocean.

His first full vintage at Pellegrini was 1992 and he continued his tenure full time through 2000, with a consulting role until 2012. Pellegrini's current winemaker is Tom Drozd.

"If I had to do it again," says Hearn. "I'd pick Pellegrini. Bob and his wife were committed to quality, and that never changed. I had all the tools and interest from ownership that … I don't think it's incorrect to say, Pellegrini was one of the main drivers that pushed Long Island to where it is now."

The Pellegrinis and Hearn wanted to focus on red wine— no riesling, rosé, or sweet wine. By 1998, they were making 10,000 cases a year and selling all of it. "We were making more merlot than Bedell," says Hearn, "and we weren't making a lot."

Like many from the early days, Hearn gives Kip Bedell a lot of credit. "His 1988 Merlot was the first best red made on Long Island," he says. "I spent a lot of time learning from him."

Hearn's first season was a weather disaster. As the guys sitting in their rocking chairs on a porch would put it: It was the year of Mount Pinatubo, a volcano in the Philippines that erupted in June 1991 and affected the weather, worldwide, for the coming year. The dispersed ash might as well have blocked the sun on Long Island, where growers got nothing but rot and unripe grapes. But sometimes the scale swings the other way; 1993, as we've learned, was the start of a string of glorious vintages for Long Island.

The first thing Hearn did was add petit verdot to the existing 28-acre vineyard, Island Vineyard, the Pellegrinis bought. They were the third winery on Long Island to make a cabernet franc and, Hearn guesses, the first to make a red blend, like the Bordeaux wines Bob Pellegrini loved and collected.

Hearn says 1993 was not only good for individual wineries, it was good for the region. "Robert Entenmann had that property [Martha Clara, a winery in Riverhead] for 40 years. He planted in '97 and '98, because some of the '93s got a lot of attention. He saw quality wine and said, 'It's time.'"

By the mid-'90s, says Hearn, Long Island Wine Country was getting a welcome transfusion of new blood. "It helped to elevate the region," he says, "and we all talked and learned from each other."

Although Hearn's main job is directing winemaking for others, he still has his own projects: two labels, Suhru, which combines his and his wife's first names and their last initial, and T'Jara, an aboriginal word that means "a sense of place," similar to the French wine term *terrior*.

Hearn and his wife own Suhru. They use only purchased fruit with the goal of featuring grapes from where they grow best in New York. Their riesling is from Gold Seal Vineyard in the Finger Lakes; the red blend, sauvignon blanc, and syrah are made from North Fork grapes. Like all of Hearn's wines, since Premium installed a dedicated bottling line in 2009, Suhru is finished under screw cap.

T'Jara is made from a vineyard the Hearns and two friends, Jed and Lori Beitler, bought in 2000 where they planted merlot, cabernet franc, cabernet sauvignon and petit verdot. He makes single varietal bottlings and in the best years a reserve, which is a blend. The first reserve was made in 2010 and sold out. Hearn passed on the less than stellar (or "challenging," as we like to say) 2011 but will create one for the 2012 and 2013 vintages already aging in tanks and barrels. "They're killer," he says. "I like to think they're at the higher echelon of Long Island wine." Hearn delivers lines like this in a voice so quiet one almost has to lean forward to hear. His warm smile prevents you from reading this as a boast. He's simply proud of what he's accomplished—which includes the two wines he chose to open for our tasting: the 1994 and 1995 Pellegrini Encore, a red blend.

"I picked '94 because while '93 and '95 were really hot, '94 was nice and warm, not really hot but really dry. The success of the 1994," says Hearn, aside from the dry vintage, can be attributed to his decision to install irrigation and to water at the beginning of the growing season. "People asked why we were irrigating," he says, "because we can get a lot of rain here in the summer. But it was so dry after bud break that the vines were starting to get stressed. A bad start like that can cause a lot of problems down the road. But after we watered, people noticed how green and unstressed the vines were. Although you don't use it very much," he adds, "irrigation is an important part of our landscape."

Another reason Hearn chose the 1994 was in 1993, he believes, a high majority of the barrels in Pellegrini's cellar were too new. "I don't think oak management was very good in 1993," he says. "In the following years, it was more integrated.

"In a new region, the first hurdle you have to get over is 'can you make good wine.' Next you have ask, 'Will they age?'" He decants the two bottles of wine into beakers from the Premium lab, pours and tilts the glass in front of a white background, and says, "This one is 20 years old. This one is 19. They don't look old."

He's right. The wines still have some of that ruby color typical of younger wine. There's minimal browning around the edge, a telltale sign of oxidation, something all wines are subject to the longer they spend in bottle. The sediment is negligible.

Hearn tastes and nods his head. "I haven't had one of these in several years," he says. "In fact, it's the last one in my cellar. But I knew at the time; I told Bob '94 was going to be one of our best wines." The '94 has higher acid. "I'm glad," says Hearn. "That was what I was hoping to show. And it showed."

The 1994 Encore was 42 percent cabernet sauvignon, 38 percent merlot, 18 percent cabernet franc and 2 percent petit verdot. In 1995 the blend was 52 percent cabernet sauvignon, 38 percent merlot, 8 percent cabernet franc and 2 percent petit verdot. As minimal as it is, the cabernet sauvignon is noticeable in the 1995, adding a smooth mouthfeel typical of cab after the tannins have dropped out due to aging. Starting in 1996, Hearn made Encore with merlot in the majority, because it ripens more consistently.

The staying power of these wines makes Hearn sanguine about his 2012s and 2013s still yet to be bottled. "Winemaking has improved since the '90s," he says. Back then there was a lot less clearing of the fruit zone, which allows rot-preventing air circulation around the fruit clusters. There was more machine harvesting, and 20 years ago, machine harvesters weren't as great as they are now.

After the tasting, some philosophy comes in. "A winemaker can be as artistic or as scientific as they want to be," he says. "For me, I'm somewhere in between, but I lean more on the scientific side. That helps me reinforce what my emotions say should be happening. Some lean too artistic, so the consistency isn't there so often. But this." He points to the wine. "This consistency of style? This is Pellegrini."

Miguel Martin: Cool Weather, Cool Varietals and Merlot

Behind the Bottle: Palmer Vineyards 2010 Old Roots Merlot

Miguel Martin, the Spanish-born winemaker at Palmer Vineyards in Aquebogue since 2006, is both a newcomer and an old-timer. He started there a year earlier than Anthony Nappa of Anomaly fame, one of the young Long Island winemakers at the crest of the wave of new talent washing ashore the East End, and one year after Kelly Urbanik Koch, of Macari, left the West Coast. Here's where it gets weird. He also spent two and a half years, starting in 1988, at Le Rêve, the Southampton winery owned by Alan Barr that is now Duck Walk. The end of the '80s was truly the time for a tight-knit pack of pioneers in Long Island Wine Country. Martin had the chance to rub elbows with Peter and Patricia Lenz, the Hargraves, Kip Bedell and Lyle Greenfield of Bridgehampton Winery. The region was barely out of its first decade of wine production and there were still a lot of things to figure out—including financing. Barr, a commercial builder in New York, would soon lose the winery to debt and troubles with the town, but the opportunity gave Martin, a graduate of the Technical University of Madrid, with a degree in agricultural engineering a chance to control a winery on his own and be part of the rearing of a new wine region.

But he didn't come to New York for that. He came to New York on an exchange program to learn English. The wine job, he says, "was pure coincidence." He arrived in February expecting to be picked up by the family he was set to stay with in Great Neck. No one came. His English was rudimentary, and there was three feet of snow on the ground. "I had the number and called," he says. "And the woman on the phone said, 'Oh, we forgot to pick you up. Just take a taxi.' I'm lucky the guy was from Puerto Rico and spoke Spanish." At the house, he says, a woman answered the door with a cigarette in her hand and cats flying, reminding him of his allergies. "She told me to go the second floor and that I would be sharing a room with another guy."

The situation got old fast, and Martin started looking for something else. Then one day he opened the paper and saw a winery in Southampton was looking for a winemaker. "I got my resume together and the guy hired me," he says. "He was desperate."

The son of an electrician, Martin was born in Córdoba, a landlocked city of 300,000 in the southern reaches of Spain and was raised in Madrid. "My father always drank wine," he says. "He had a glass of white wine for lunch and one for dinner. I grew up seeing wine on the dining table, and for me, wine was more like another ingredient added to the meal." But that was the extent of it; there was no social drinking outside the family table, and no family members in the wine business. Spain has a rich history of winemaking, but it all but stopped progressing during the years the dictator Francisco Franco was in power; outside influence was moribund and the prospect of exporting wine was nigh impossible. Franco's death in 1975 ushered a new hope for the industry and revived family vineyards as the younger generation gradually took over and brought the wines to the global stage.

Not being a member of one of those families, Martin did not imagine a wine career was in his future. "Winemaking in

Spain is passed from one generation to another," he says, his voice still inflected with an Andalusian accent. "Even if you never went to school for it or if you hate wines. It was more like tradition." So his choice to attend the Madrid's Technical University was a matter of convenience, and his choice to study agriculture was one of preference. "I wanted to do something with soil and farming," he says. "And, almost naturally, one of the studies was fermentation science." For the agriculture degree, Martin needed to finish four years of general study and then three years in a chosen field. Within fermentation science is winemaking, which captured his attention. In the past, he says, there were few such programs; most training in the wine business was for students who didn't want to go to a university but wished to become cellar hands.

His sights were bigger, and his next move was to Galicia, the most northwestern region of Spain, where he worked harvest. Galicia is the home of the light, peachy, aromatic, zesty grape variety of albariño, a cool climate grape if there ever was one. "I fell in love with it," says Martin.

Galicia's cool climate is due to its northern clime, but also because it borders the Atlantic Ocean, like Long Island. In 2008—as mentioned in the introduction—the now-defunct Stony Brook Center for Food, Wine and Culture sponsored a symposium called the Art of Balance: Cool Climate/Maritime Wines in a Global Context, which sought to bring together producers from regions with growing conditions similar to Long Island; Rias Baixas, as the wine region in Galicia is known, was one of them.

The connection had already been made for Martin, even if he didn't quite know how it would turn out. After that harvest in Rias Baixas, he landed on the steps of a cat lady in Great Neck.

"I met the other winemakers," he says. "At that time Wölffer was called Sagaponack Winery, but I always had on my mind to stay here a couple of years and get enough money to go to UC [Davis] to get my master's." Between jobs at local restaurants and the winery and meeting his future wife, Martin soon had enough money and English language skills to make the move to California.

After completing his degree, Martin started on a whirlwind world tour of wine regions that started in the cellars of Gloria Ferrer in Sonoma, where he lived the life of a lab rat measuring pH and alcohol content. The next stop was Yalumba in Australia, where he was able to visit New Zealand, then to Chile where he got his first hands-on winemaking job at Caliterra. Then it was back to California and a job as winemaker at the Mondavi brand Woodbridge. Then back to Spain to the Penedès region and a job helping to build a new winery for the Spanish wine behemoth González Byass.

But then, back in Southampton, one of his wife's sisters picked up the paper and saw Palmer Vineyards was looking for a winemaker. Martin sent his resume, flew to New York to interview in August, and was hired on the spot. "Bob [Palmer] said I was the best of five candidates to take Palmer to the next level." His wife was happy to be back near her four sisters; he started September 1.

He wasn't coming back to unfamiliar territory. His family had returned to Southampton each summer to visit his wife's family, and he had kept up with the wines. "I've seen the evolution of the region and the fine tuning of what grows best, and the fine tuning of the wines," he says. "As soon as you know where the grapes grow best, to maximize the potential of the grapes—the varietal components of the grapes—that's when you start making good wine."

As the winemakers learned this, Martin says, there's been a better understanding between vineyard managers and winemakers. "In general," he says, "we have elevated the quality of the grapes, because the winemakers are demanding better quality fruit. It's not just 'bring me grapes,' now it's 'bring me the best cabernet franc.'"

And Martin inherited a lot of grapes. Palmer, one of the more western vineyards on the North Fork—where the growing season is longer and warmer—had 90 acres planted with merlot, chardonnay, sauvignon blanc, gewürztraminer, cabernet sauvignon and cabernet franc and was one of two vineyards on the North Fork to grow pinot blanc.

For the first two years, he says, he tried to maintain the style and techniques of departing winemaker Tom Drozd, a veteran of the East End, who now works at Pellegrini and Baiting Hollow Farm Vineyard. But it didn't feel right. "I thought 'wow, what am I doing?'" he says. "I'm going to plant albariño; I'm going to made the sauvignon blanc different." That revelation resulted in the planting in 2007 of albariño, muscat and malvasia. "I really wanted to put my signature on my wines," he says. "Think about a chef in a new restaurant. He doesn't want to keep too much of the old menu. They used to have cream of broccoli with potatoes. I'm going to change that, I'm going to make cream of carrots." He adds he believes in evolution, not revolution. "I didn't want it to be all of a sudden; I wanted to start with leaving the wine longer in barrels and using longer maceration. And in general, I'm really happy. People are responding well to the changes; we're almost caught up on vintages, and we're sold out of many wines." Accounts call him, he says, just asking to send five cases of sauvignon blanc. "They say they don't need to taste it, they know it's going to be good." And Martin's sauvignon blanc is good. If you're looking for the hyper-grassy style associated with New Zealand, look elsewhere. The wine is somewhere in between Sancerre—the French wine region that dictated the grape's style for centuries before the first sauvignon blanc went into the ground in Marlborough in 1973, the same year, as we know, the first wine grapes were planted on the East End—and New Zealand. It's crisp, rich with minor hints of grass and major hints of citrus fruit. Just right for a region in between the two that is putting the fine points on the definition of its place in the world of wine.

Martin's planting of those aromatic grapes in 2007, the first on Long Island, is a tip toward revolution, but in a small way. He only had one acre, and the sum of the first release in 2010 was 30 cases of 500 milliliter bottles. Plans to add three more acres are in the works. The wine was very well received and sold out quickly. Subsequent vintages have been as successful, reaching the zesty peachiness of Galicia, without the saline qualities sometimes present. Palmer's Albariño is more firmly planted in the vineyard's gravely soil than the windswept promontory of Rias Biaxas.

This incremental change in winery production doesn't blind Martin to what the North Fork does best: merlot. The grape loves the soil, has enough time to ripen and ripens gradually, due to our cool climate. Here wine from merlot stands squarely between the high alcohol merlots of California with a slight lean toward the right bank in Bordeaux, where it is the major component of Pomerol and Saint-Émilion. Like Bordeaux, Long Island can be subject to devastating storms during harvest season, but the wine there, like here, is made to be a subtle savory accompaniment to food. And in a great year, like 2010, the fruit in merlot sings and its medium tannins can make the wine ready for early drinking. This is why Martin chose a new bottling, the 2010 Old Roots Merlot, released in 2014, to feature. Again, he's somewhere in the middle: The wine was made to be ready to drink upon release, but it wasn't released right away, as some lighter versions can be.

"Merlot, with cab franc, is the signature of Long Island," says Martin. "I think merlot is the grape for the history books. The Long Island wine industry and merlot are, like, side by side. You can't talk about it without mentioning merlot and chardonnay."

The 2010 Old Roots Merlot, the first of its name, sells for $42 in the tasting room and will age from four to five years, says Martin. But the magic in it is the 2010 growing season, the best so far this decade until 2013, and 2014, came along. "It was an extraordinary year," he says. "And in years like that, you can almost elevate the varietal, so that when people taste the wine, it's really unexpected merlot. It's beautiful and unique. And helps them recognize the importance of this grape varietal; it deserves the attention it deserves."

The most useful part of a great growing season is that it gives vineyard managers and winemakers choices. There's no last-minute rush to get the grapes in before a hurricane comes barreling up the Eastern Seaboard. "You have the luxury of waiting to pick," says Martin. The idea for Old Roots, he adds, came after the harvest when he was tasting separate barrels in preparation for blending. "And I tasted one that was really beautiful, with a mocha-cherry balance, so I marked those barrels, and they were all coming from the older vineyards, which were planted 30 years ago," he says. "So when I was done tasting, I had eight barrels that were really unique." He went back and tasted each barrel to define their strongest attributes. Some had richer tannins, others emphasized the fruit and mouthfeel, and another had a long-lingering finish or an aroma that jumped out of the glass.

He selected a few gallons from each barrel to make a blend, one that would knit together the all the desired qualities, and ended up with three full barrels; all the wine had gone through the same vinification process: unfiltered; the same yeast; 18 percent new French oak medium toast; and two and a half years in barrel.

"The color is really beautiful," says Martin. "And it really shows on the nose that it was a ripe year. When you pick it up, you can almost feel the weight in the glass. This is no wishy-washy wine." He checks the aroma. "I get mocha, chocolate, caramel, toffee. The fruit is there. You can see it's a warm year: a little prune juice and black cherry. The mouth is very textural, with elastic tannins, not aggressive at all. I love how this wine coats your whole mouth, which makes the wine very persistent with a long beautiful finish; you don't need to rush to get a second sip. It retains the aromatics and the flavors."

Martin adds, "I love this wine right now. I don't know if it will last for my grandkids, but I assembled it for the present; you will see some changes in three or four years, but I don't know if those changes are going to be positive or decrease the quality of the wine. I have nothing to compare it with."

He puts down the glass. "My intention is to enjoy it right now. It's a 2010. It's already four years old. I don't make wines like Eric Fry."

Gilles Martin: From the Gate of Champagne to Sparkling Pointe

Behind the Bottle: Sparkling Pointe 2005 Brut Seduction

The bottling line is clanking away, clearly audible in the open white tasting room of Sparkling Pointe in Southold. Gilles Martin, the winemaker, is distracted, leaning toward the clatter. "I can tell if it's not working by the sound," he says in his thick French accent. He's granted a few hours to sit down during bottling season, which at Sparkling Pointe takes three weeks in the late spring; when things are going full tilt, the line can fill 2,400 bottles per hour. "If it's not going right," he says, "it goes down to 1,200." He's clearly got a schedule, and the three people manning the mechanized bottling line surely know it. They are filling wire crates with the thick bottles used expressly for sparkling wine, strong enough to withstand without bursting the in-bottle second fermentation that creates the bubbles.

This is the first stage of making sparkling wine. A base wine is pumped into bottles with a small amount of yeast and sugar and topped with a crown cap. The yeast, which eats the sugar and in turn produces alcohol and carbon dioxide, will do its work over the summer. When the wine is ready for sale, the workers will return to the bottling line to expel the dead yeast and pop in the distinctive cork used to top sparkling wine and secure it with a wire cage.

This method of getting bubbles into wine was created, legend has it, by accident by the Benedictine monk Dom Pérignon. Less time-consuming and expensive ways of injecting bubbles into wine have been invented since, either by doing the second fermentation in bulk or gassing the wine like soda. Martin calls the way he does it Méthode Champenoise; the

Champenois prefer the term *méthode traditionelle,* so jealously do they guard the use of the name Champagne. It's not illegal to call sparkling wine Champagne in the United States, but a large majority of domestic producers respect the wishes of the French and call their cuvées *sparkling wine.* It's a little clunkier but, hey, what are you going to do?

Martin untwists the wine cage on a bottle of his 2005 Brut Seduction, what the French would call his *tête de cuvee,* a sparkler made only in years that have a certain *je ne sais quoi.* It's something he can come close to describing, relying on vague terms that, when they come out of his mouth, sound precise.

"It's a unique blend of chardonnay and pinot noir," he says. But what can be *unique* about blending chardonnay and pinot noir? Were the grapes especially ripe?

"It's not only the ripeness," he answers with the slightest hint of impatience. "It's the quality of the base wine, a balance of acidity and alcohol that reaches that harmony." And the wine must have the ability to age; the 2005 is nine years old, he points out, and still tastes fresh.

"It's a unique cuvee that can perform that long," he says. "You have to have that knowledge and memory to put it together year after year, but in certain years only." One benefit of growing grapes for sparkling wine on Long Island, he says, is that the climate is not as difficult as it is in Champagne, where the short growing season dictates the style of the wine.

Without having really explained his process, he gives up and tastes. "This is very sophisticated wine," he says. "They never had wine like this on the East Coast."

Essentially he is telling me the proof is in the bottle, stop overthinking it.

Martin was born in Meaux, an agricultural region just northeast of Paris that he calls the gate to Champagne. His grandfather, after suffering the pollution of early 20th-century Paris, moved back to his roots, an apple orchard in Meaux, where he made cider. "The pear is the queen of fruits," says Martin, "but the apple is king." The family had apples year round, storing them in a cellar because they had no refrigeration. "There was one, the *pomme du moissonneur*, what is the word for that, when you cut the wheat," he asks. A quick Google search turns up "reaper." "Like Jack the Ripper," he asks. Not quite. With that cleared up, he explains it was the apple ripe for the picking when the reapers were doing their work.

Wine did run in the family; an uncle was a winemaker who worked in a research station in the south of France run by the government. And wine was always on the table, from Alsace, where part of his family was from, and the rest of the France: Bordeaux, the Loire Valley and Burgundy. But the first vineyards he ever saw were in Champagne.

In school he gravitated toward the sciences, biology in particular, and graduated with a diploma in technology from the University of Paris focusing on the food industry and biotechnology. His first job out of school was at General Foods where they were developing the first sugarless chewing gum. He was happy with the job but wanted to get a master's. His uncle said, "Why not enology?"

"He was the one who wet my feet in the pommace," says Martin. So he moved south to Montpelier and its university, where the degree took two and a half years. At the end he was recognized for having written the best master's thesis in the country—on cold filtration—in a ceremony conducted by President Jacques Chirac. But, he missed it. He was working an internship in Australia, because he wanted to be fluent in English.

"It was a bad place to go to learn proper English," he says, but he did see a side of industrial winemaking completely foreign to a Frenchman. "It was unbelievable that the grapes were coming from 400 miles away," he says. Another internship, in Germany, taught about the country's tradition of riesling. He went back to France for an extended internship at the INRA, the National Institute for Agricultural Research, followed by a job as a consultant in a lab that served 25 wineries in Nîmes, in the south of France.

"My feet were now dark purple with the grapes," he says. "It was also fantastic that I started in a year that was quite rainy. It was an eye opener. I learned a lot of tricks when it comes to winemaking in a bad weather year."

Martin was itching to travel, and one of his former professors knew it; he told him about a winery in Virginia, Oasis, that was looking for a winemaker. The lab didn't match the offer, so in 1988 Martin left for the States, where he would finally settle. (Oasis made the news in 2009 when its owner, Tareq Salahi, and his ex-wife, Michaele crashed a state dinner at the White House.) In Virginia, Martin worked with French wine grapes as well as American hybrids. "It was a beautiful area," he says, "but after two years, I realized the whole wine industry was in California." Through his uncle, he had a connection with Roederer Estate in the Anderson Valley, a sparkling wine house started by the French winery Louis Roederer. "I called him and then took my car and drove across the States," he says. "They told me if I wanted a job to get my paperwork done. I drove back to Virginia and then took a vacation in France while I waited for my visa." Paperwork in hand, he returned to Virginia, packed his car and drove west.

Martin's six years at Roederer started in 1990. Even though the winery made only sparkling wine, one year a still wine from pinot noir was so good they released it.

"I enjoyed my time there," he says, "but have you ever been to Anderson Valley? The people are born there, they live there and they die there, or they move." While at Roederer, Martin had the opportunity to visit the North Fork, trying to sell bulk wine during an economic downturn. He did some business with Pindar and was able to try some of the wines. "In the early '90s, it was still a bit rough out here," he says. "But the '93s were the first best wines I had."

Roederer is an independent part of a company that includes the Champagne house of Deutz, and Delas, a winery in the Rhone Valley. Martin's next move was to Delas; during that time he met his French wife, a linguistics professor at Rutgers in New Jersey. For a few years she tried to find a job in France but could not. Through the industry Martin found out about a job at Macari and started in 1997. "That's how I ended up on Long Island," he says.

In 2000, he moved to Martha Clara, just helping out with their sparkling and dessert wines. At the time, not many wineries on Long Island were making sparkling wine. Lenz always has, and so did Pindar. He also started consulting with Sherwood House, where he still serves as winemaker, and Broadfields, a vineyard established in Southold in 1997 that was sold in 2005 to Napa Valley investors and then ripped out. Martha Clara makes all its wine at Premium Wine Group, the custom crush operation in Mattituck owned in part by Russell Hearn. There, Martin started to work with Hearn and met newcomers to Long Island Wine Country wishing to start their own labels. By 2002, he had taken over as winemaker at Martha Clara, where he stayed until 2007. Next stop: Sparkling Pointe.

The vineyards at Sparkling Pointe were planted in 2004, and Martin had a hand in choosing the varieties and clones to plant. Cynthia and Tom Rosicki, attorneys with offices on Long Island, in the Hudson Valley and western New York State, had contacted Steve Mudd, the man who has planted numerous local vineyards, telling him they wanted to plant their own. "Steve asked them what they liked to drink," says Martin. "And they said 'Champagne.' He told them 'This is what you do. You plant a sparkling vineyard, and I know the exact person you should do it with.

"It was a great idea," says Martin. "The Rosickis approached me and said they'd like me to make the best sparkling wine; we like your style. No one on Long Island would want to do that. They have guts, that's for sure. No one else is committed as we are to sparkling wine. And if visitors don't know that much about Champagne or sparkling, and then they come here? It's a winning situation."

Martin and Mudd decided to only plant the three varieties permitted to be used for Champagne: chardonnay, pinot noir and pinot meunier. To acquire the vines, the men used cuttings from vineyards where Martin had already used the grapes. "I knew exactly what I was getting started with," he says. The vines were French clones; early on, Long Island vineyard managers planted clones from California. The years have proved French clones produce better wine in the local climate. The Rosickis also gave Martin carte blanche when they added a winery to the property; he was able to build what he believed was needed to make great wine.

Originally, the Rosickis planted 10 acres on their property on the North Road, across the street from some of the Mudd family's original vineyards. When Ray Blum, the founder of Peconic Bay and Ackerly Pond wineries, died, the Rosickis added his 17 acres. Next, four more acres of chardonnay, pinot noir and pinot meunier—the real stuff, says Martin—will be planted next to the original 10.

Hopefully they will help to add to the production of Brut Seduction, a brand Martin created before he started working at Sparkling Pointe; 2005 is the first time he made it there. That vintage was a roller coaster of emotion for vineyard managers and winemakers alike. By late September, everyone was practically giddy with expectation. The summer had been so hot and so dry; the grapes were pristine, all they had to do was hold on until the end of October and be picked at optimum ripeness and health. Then the sky opened. Starting Columbus Day weekend, it started raining and didn't stop until a week and 17 inches later; some wineries weathered the deluge, others lost a considerable amount of fruit. It was a good year to be in the sparkling wine business, which can start picking in the last days of August. The early harvest takes into account the desire to keep alcohol levels low; the secondary fermentation, which creates the bubbles and boosts the alcohol content of the wine. But earlier harvested grapes have higher acid levels. Thus, the winemaker must consider *dosage*, the last addition to sparkling wine made in the traditional method before corking. Dosage is a mixture of reserve wine and sugar syrup designed to fill the space left by disgorgement—the expellment of the dead yeast cells—and to balance the natural acidity of the wine. Martin says dosage is the way to polish the style of a cuvée.

And if there were a word for the 2005 Brut Seduction, it would be "polished." "There's a fruitiness," says Martin. "A doughiness, like brioche. The bubbles are very tiny, ticklish on the palate, but distinctive." He adds, "There's elegance, and a balance with the fruit profile, the acidity and aroma." He credits the traditional method with giving the wine a deep structure due to the yeasty character.

This is where I tell you not to save sparkling wine for a special occasion. Martin and Sparkling Pointe produce a range of wines at a range of prices to serve as aperitifs and to complement a assortment of dishes including shellfish, seafood and white meat, like veal and pork. The younger wines have a fruitiness, like the apples of Martin's youth, but the Brut

Seduction has something more. In 2009, Martin entered his 2000 vintage, made before he joined Sparkling Pointe, in the San Francisco *Chronicle*'s annual wine competition. It took best in class. "There's a lot of American competition there," he says. "It really put us on the map." And the honor secured his place as a premiere sparkling winemaker, which he credits to the time he spent with Roederer and the years he went back to Champagne to help with the blending and finishing of wine for Louis Roederer and Deutz.

"My winemaking style is Gallic," he says. "I'm French born, raised and educated." •

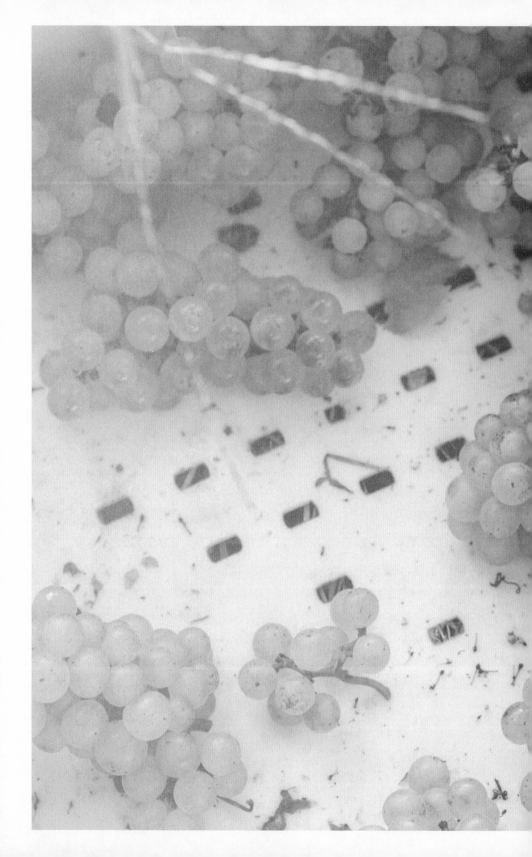

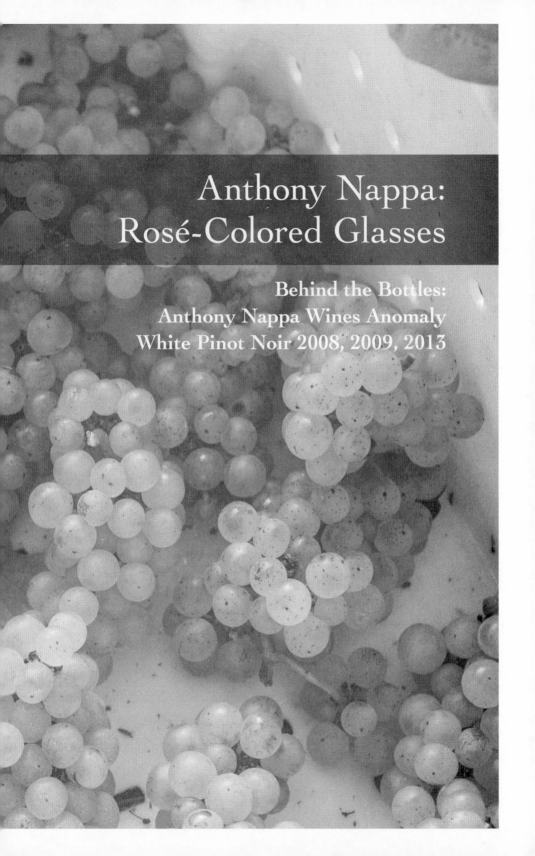

Anthony Nappa:
Rosé-Colored Glasses

Behind the Bottles:
Anthony Nappa Wines Anomaly
White Pinot Noir 2008, 2009, 2013

Long Island made one of its biggest nationwide splashes in 1995 when the *Wine Spectator* called Kip Bedell of Bedell Cellars in Cutchogue "Long Island's Master of Merlot." The next local winemaker we might see the magazine acknowledging his mastery would be Anthony Nappa with the sobriquet "The Master of White Pinot Noir." Doesn't quite roll off the tongue the same way, but hear me out. No one wine has made as much of a splash in terms of popularity and buzz as Anomaly, the salmon-tinted sipper Nappa debuted in 2009. It was one of the first to have a non-wine name and be made by a member of the new generation of winemakers that has come to the East End to show they can make good wine; they already know Long Island can. Proving that is a thing of the past.

"I've always been interested in Long Island wine," says Nappa, a Massachusetts native and graduate of the winemaking program at Lincoln University in Christchurch, New Zealand. In fact, he says, he sent e-mails and made phone calls to Russell Hearn of Premium Wine Group years ago looking for work and never heard back. "He probably doesn't even remember it," he says. His breakthrough was a posting on winejobs.com for a winemaker at Shinn Estate Vineyards, where he started with the 2007 vintage. And like so many who come out to wine country to work, he ended up staying, marrying and having a baby.

No one in Nappa's immediate family was in the wine business. His father grew up in Italy, where the family had a vineyard, but neither of his parents really drink that much wine, he says. "On special occasions, or whatever." But at his public high school he was drawn to science and math and in summers worked on some local farms. This led to enrollment at the Stockbridge School of Agriculture at UMass Amherst, but not until after a backpacking hiatus in Europe, where he spent a lot of time in Italy and was exposed to the wine culture. "I didn't have much direction," he says. "And I couldn't go to school for no reason." But when he got back, his mother put her foot down: It was time to go to college. But Nappa had to pay for it himself, so he went back to work to save for ag school.

UMass is a land grant college, so agriculture education is a priority. The oldest buildings are the ag buildings, says Nappa, but the enrollment is small; only 150 students were in the program. He studied plant science with a focus on fruits and vegetables. "Most people studied turf so they could go to work at a golf course," he says. "Or landscape design. But by the time I got out of school there was no money in ag." It was 2000, so he got into construction, painting houses and roofing. Soon he had his own company. "It was boom times," he says, "but then 9/11 happened and it was over. It was like a light switch; all jobs got cancelled, and I had to fire everybody. No one wanted to do home improvements anymore."

But before the crash he was able to travel one more time. An old application for a semester at sea came through and soon he was on a boat navigating the world. Events interrupted again. The USS *Cole* was bombed in Yemen, cancelling a trip through the Suez Canal. Instead, the ship stopped for a week in Stellenbosch, South Africa, where Nappa once again encountered wine, taking the time to visit tasting rooms. There the thought entered his mind: I should go to school for this. The question was *where*. He liked that English was spoken in South Africa, but the rand was weak, and UC Davis was too expensive for an out-of-stater. Where else to go? New Zealand, which he had visited in past travels. "I got in," he says. "And they said 'You can come this semester if you want.'" So after cashing out of the construction company, he started in May 2002, which is harvest time south of the equator. "I sold my trucks," he says. "Then I had enough to pay for college." He worked the harvests and there met Sarah Evans, a fellow American student studying animal science with a focus on horses. The two would end up marrying on Long Island.

At Lincoln, where he studied viticulture, Nappa's housing was near the school's vineyards and wineries. "We made wine all the time," he says. "I could use the lab whenever I wanted." That was when he found he was good at winemaking. "I had a good palate and was good at the chemistry of it." He adds, "The chemistry on the wine side was a little harder."

This is a pattern for many of the Long Island winemakers. Unsure, or intimidated about the skills and knowledge needed to make wine, they start by studying viticulture because they love plants and being outside, and it's a way to stay close to the business. But as their learning curve increases, and the prospect no longer seems so scary, the lure of the cellar overpowers that of the vineyard. Which is not to say viticulture training is not worthwhile. Good winemakers walk the rows with their vine-yard managers nearly every day.

Some part of a learning winemaker's life is chasing the harvest, and the advantage of two hemispheres is that you can do it twice a year if you're willing to travel. Nappa was, and his interest in Long Island wine led him to apply to work at Paumanok Vineyards in Aquebogue, one of Long Island's more established wineries. That year, it didn't work out. He had been away from home for a long time, so he instead went to a sparkling wine house in Massachusetts, Westport Rivers, where they also make a white pinot noir.

After a time, he returned to school, finished his degree, worked a few more harvests and then hit the road for one last tour, this time in Southeast Asia before moving to Campagnia, Italy, to work for a winery that was modernizing. "They were nice people," he says. "And I liked it there." But soon the folks at another Massachusetts winery were calling; they had heard about him from the people at Westport Rivers. It was a brand new project. "A clean slate," Nappa says, one that gave him a lot of experience in starting a winery but in an unorganized fashion. "I was buying a lot of equipment at the last minute," he says, "and making wine, but it wasn't real; it wasn't true." The winery didn't make it. "They never finished it," he says. "They weren't millionaires, like out here."

The following spring, 2006, he went back to applying for jobs, and back to New Zealand to work the harvest. There he worked in a custom crush operation that was so big, he says, he had no responsibility. "I'd leave work, get drunk, hang out, whatever," he says. Once harvest was finished in May, he turned back to New York and made that call to Russell Hearn, thinking he had an in because he knew Eric Fry, the winemaker at the Lenz Winery, who had worked as a consultant for Westport Rivers.

No luck that time. But California called, and he was offered a job in another huge custom crush winery. "In one winery," he says, "they were doing three times the amount of wine Long Island even makes." The pay was good, housing was included, as was a phone and a car, so he said yes. "Then, the day after I said 'yes' Russell Hearn called," says Nappa. "I had to tell him 'sorry.'"

He spent the 2006 California harvest working in that winery, which had every toy in the book, and was going 24/7. "I saw a lot of crazy stuff," he says. "My boss, who was head winemaker, he didn't know he was the head winemaker until the business cards showed up." Still, it was interesting and fun, but by spring 2007, he was burned out. "I interviewed for jobs up and down California," he says. "There was nothing. Not one." Then he spotted that ad on winejobs.com for a winemaker at Shinn Estate Vineyards. "I have this feeling things happen for a reason," he says. "And you have to be able to take opportunities. When I moved to California, I was replacing an Italian guy, and he gave me a copy of Louisa Hargrave's book." This is the same Louisa Hargrave we met in the first chapter who, with her former husband Alex, planted the first European grape vines on Long Island. "I read it," Nappa says.

Boom, he landed just in time for the 2007 harvest, a fantastic vintage. Boom, he was working with Roman Roth, who was consulting at Shinn and who is one of the more experienced winemakers on Long Island, having started at Wölffer Estate Vineyard on the South Fork in 1992. Nappa had two conditions: to be able to start his own brand and to bring his dog to work. Done.

The stint at Shinn lasted four years, and Nappa's label, Anthony Nappa Wines, released its first bottling the next spring: 200 cases of a red pinot noir called Nemesis with grapes from the Martha Clara vineyards.

"When I first started making my own wine, I thought it'd be something small, a couple of cases on the side," he says. "But it ended up growing into something much bigger." He was happy working with pinot noir, which can be tricky on the East End. "It's one of those grapes that gives you a window into a region quickly; it's very transparent." And in 2007 he had a lot to work with. It was a dry, steadily warm season, and the wine turned out so well he signed up to buy the same fruit next year.

But the next year's growing season wasn't so great—damp and cool—and Nappa found himself in possession of a bunch of pinot noir that wasn't as ripe or as clean as the previous year's batch. As a man without a vineyard, he wanted to honor his contract and be a good customer, so he took the grapes and recalled the wines made at Westport Rivers in Massachusetts, where they turned pinot noir into sparkling wine (as they do in Champagne) and into a still white wine. It seemed like a one-off thing, so Nappa and his soon-to-be wife, Sarah, named it Anomaly and crossed their fingers. One hundred and eighty cases were released in spring 2009 and by August it was gone, sold out of the tasting room at Shinn for $18. "I never thought it would happen again," he says.

After meeting in New Zealand, Nappa and Evans kept in touch. After spending a few years traveling and teaching English, she returned to the States and went to culinary school.

She too found her way to the East End and started working in the kitchen at North Fork Table and Inn, one of the region's premiere restaurants, when serendipity struck again. Nappa was leaving Shinn but wasn't able to find a job that would allow him to keep his own label. There was nothing left to do but strike out on his own. That was when a cooperative tasting room on Peconic Lane, run by Theresa Dilworth, winemaker and owner of Comtesse Thérèse, came up for sale. The tiny storefront in the tiny commercial zone of the tiny hamlet of Peconic had already been established as a stop on the wine trail, and plenty of other winemakers with their own labels wanted a place where their wine could be featured. This included Roman Roth, with his Grapes of Roth label and Russell Hearn, who was releasing two, Suhru and T'Jara. Christened the Winemaker Studio, the tasting room soon became a hangout for the younger generation of winemakers and workers in the wine business. Evans quit her job and took over the store in 2011. "There was almost a year and a half when neither of us had a salary," says Nappa. "We paid ourselves an hourly wage."

Nappa kept expanding his portfolio with wines like riesling, gewürztraminer, chardonnay and a big merlot, each with their own names: Spezia for the spicy gewürz; Sciardonné for the chard; and Blackbird for his merlot. A lot of this was possible due to Anomaly, which did happen again, and again. They upped production to 250 cases and by the 2009 vintage were making 900 cases. In 2013 they released 1,200 cases of the 2012 vintage. Nappa was now sourcing grapes from upstate as well as Long Island. But money was still not flowing in, and in January 2013, Nappa was hired to take over winemaking at Raphael, which gave him a salary and a place to make Anthony Nappa Wines.

From 5 to 7 p.m. Friday to Sunday, the Winemaker Studio holds a happy hour with 30 percent off glasses of wine; on Mondays visitors get 50 percent off. With the positive changes in New York State liquor laws, Nappa and Evans are now able to serve any alcoholic beverage made in the state. Local beer is on tap, and one can get a flight of locally produced spirits and taste the range of whiskeys coming out of Long Island Spirits, where vodka, bourbon and liqueurs are distilled. In 2012 in an attached storefront, the couple opened Provisions, which sells charcuterie, local products and bottled beer. Happy hour is busy.

In 2014 during happy hour, with new baby, Primo, in tow, Nappa opened a 2008 and a 2009 Anomaly, along with the just-bottled 2013. The wines are made to be drunk young, and the older vintages were showing their age; the salmon pink had turned a salmon brown, but Nappa still found things to learn from their development. "It's lost its fruit," he says. "A little over the hill, but it could be bottle variation." He adds, "It's interesting. Old wines are always interesting. We taste verticals of all the wines to put them in context."

What he's looking for is consistency year after year, which requires work in the vineyard and the winery when growing seasons vary, as they do on Long Island. "We can do it, by managing when we pick," he says, "and buying grapes when they're available from different regions.

"We pick on flavor, trying to hit the same profile of strawberry and white cherry," he says. "The only thing that changes is the color, which I can remove with carbon. In 2012, it was more pink, more rosy." He's also learned how to blend upstate and island fruit. "The Finger Lakes is acid driven," he says. "Here is more fruit driven." In either case, the wine does not need super ripe fruit from a super dry year to be successful. "If it's a bad year, people call me," he says. "If it's rotting in the third week of September, people know I'll take it. Pinot lends itself to being a white wine so well, with a natural balance of aromatics, and it's so light and fruity. Pinot doesn't need oak."

What he's making is a stripped-down pinot noir that's a great all around wine, very approachable with nothing but fruit to define it. He did once try to make a barrel-fermented reserve Anomaly, he says, "but it just doesn't work."

Adam Suprenant:
From Candy Counter
to Candy Counter

Behind the Bottle:
Coffee Pot Cellars 2008 Merlot

Adam Suprenant has been flying under the radar for years. Just ask him about it. He'll present you with printouts showing the medals and scores his wine has won in the 10 years since he became the winemaker at Osprey's Dominion in Peconic. *The Wine Spectator* gave his 2007 Reserve Merlot 90 points and the 2007 Cabernet Sauvignon an 89. In May 2013, *Wine Enthusiast* gave his 2012 Fume Blanc an 89 and his 2007 Flight, a red blend, an 89. The winery, which began producing its own wine in 1992, (the infamous vintage affected by the eruption of Mount Pinatubo) and opened its tasting room in 1994, is a popular place with many visitors and has an extensive list of wine, but it hasn't really caught on as a brand like some of its Main Road neighbors such as Bedell or Lenz. It's OK though; Suprenant is happy with what he's doing and how he's doing it. Osprey's was the first winery to install a windmill, has been using bio-diesel for almost a decade and has made low level spraying a part of its viticulture, as well as planting clover as a cover crop to fix nitrogen levels for just as long. "We call it 'doing the right thing,'" he says. But he still declines to join Long Island Sustainable Winegrowing, a group formed by some wineries in 2012 to formalize best practices to protect the aquifer and limit the amount of chemicals while making winegrowing sustainable for the workers and the land.

"Doing the right thing is now being called sustainable," he says. "I don't believe in the term. It's the wrong word and you shouldn't give yourself an award for doing that." He adds that the requirements for being certified by LISW are not comprehensive and that "sustainable" is a marketing term. "I don't think the consumer is really that dialed-in to sustainability as a marketing thing for wine," he says. "They're more interested in quality, and sustainability is no guarantee that you make better wine."

Under the radar? More like outside the tracking system in the current environment. He also still uses the term Meritage, a formalized quality standard for red blends that was popular at the turn of the century. So he's not a joiner, but he is. He makes numerous wines, including a spiced wine that does a lot to help out sales in off years. No one really does that anymore, but Osprey's does and keeps selling out. Suprenant is unapologetic. He stands behind his wine, and the winery's business plan, while semi-quietly going about making strong merlots, complex blends and vinifying the most varietals on Long Island, which at 13 includes pinot gris, tannant and carmenere.

Like many of the winemakers on Long Island, Suprenant came to his profession in a roundabout way. He was turned on to wine by his father, a "big wine hobbyist," who was an active member of the International Wine & Food Society and kept a cellar when Suprenant was a growing up in Bronxville, an affluent suburb north of New York City. The drinking age was lower then, so once Suprenant turned 18, he accompanied his father to tastings in Manhattan. "I went to formal dinners and got a taste of the great '76 *trockenbeerenausleses* from Germany," he says.

Suprenant would characterize his time in high school as being somewhere among a jock (he wrestled), a nerd (a student court judge) and a stoner. But he always liked science. He went to SUNY Morrisville for two years and then transferred to Cornell, where he would graduate with a degree in plant science. It wasn't too far afield; his father's side of the family worked 33 acres in South Salem, N.Y. The original farm was in Manhattan near Columbia University until development pressured them to move. The farm, which was passed down to his father and his cousin, traded in apples and dairy. "We were renowned countywide for hard cider during Prohibition, which was made using a wooden cider press from 1870 that had to be run by a tractor motor," Suprenant says. But development reached South Salem when IBM moved headquarters to Armonk. "And then there was the Reagan recession," he adds, "which certain historians have forgotten happened." Taxes went up and the farm was sold while he was in school. (Trivia: one of the farm's outbuildings was sold to Woody Allen's production company and ended up on the set of the 1982 film "A Midsummer Night's Sex Comedy.") "I wish I knew what happened to that cider press," he says.

In hindsight, he says the farm was not suitable for grapes, and his study at Cornell was apple based; when he was there they did not offer a wine program. "There was one course in viticulture and that was it," he says. But wine called anyway.

In 1986, once he was out of school, Suprenant landed a job at Villa Banfi in Old Brookville on Long Island with the help of Peter Max F. Sichel, whose family owned the Blue Nun brand of German wine. Suprenant calls him his mentor and was one of the people he and his father met at International Wine

& Food Society tastings. "He developed Blue Nun from an obscure German wine into one of the most successful imports," says Suprenant. "He changed a stodgy, hard to read label, in that Gothic type, put a nun on it, and people really went for it." At Banfi, he worked with Fred Frank, the nephew, of Dr. Konstantin Frank of Vinifera Wine Cellars in the Finger Lakes, who was the vineyard manager.

In an example of how small the East Coast wine world is, Eric Fry of Lenz had started at Vinifera the year before as winemaker. Suprenant was hired to work in the field. "The romantic term would be viticulturist," he says. "Unfortunately, they planted a lot of the grapes in a frost pocket." But, since he was not from a vineyard background, he appreciated the opportunity to learn how things worked in the real world. A planned winery didn't work out, so Suprenant moved to retail, working at Sherry-Lehmann, a posh wine store in the city. "They had a great program," he says. "They took on young eager apprentices and gave them a wine education." At the time, says Suprenant, Sherry-Lehmann barely had any California wine on the shelves. "The U.S. wine market was not interested in U.S. wine," he says. "It was at the beginning of the California fine wine revolution."

His next job was as a rep in New York City for a Spanish wine importer, Joseph Victori, slinging the bag, as they say, doing tastings for retailers and restaurants to get the wines on the shelves and on lists. His wares included Marqués de Riscal and Codorniu, established brands. But it also included a fading craze, the wine cooler. "Remember Calvin Coolers," he asks. "With the tag line 'Wine is fine, but Calvin's is cooler?'"

The rep thing didn't work out. Suprenant found himself knocking on the doors of shops with bulletproof windows, where he felt uncomfortable in his Brooks Brothers suit. From there he went into another side of the wine world, working as a waiter in French restaurants and joining the union; he eventually became a shop steward. But he found it unsatisfying, even with the number of celebrities he waited on. After five years, he pooled his money, applied to UC Davis's wine program and went back to school in 1992.

His education included internships at Trefethen and Piper Sonoma and a harvest season at Chateau Lafite Rothschild, which takes one Davis student each year. He specialized in sensory science, working under professor Ann Noble, who invented the aroma wheel, a standard for wine descriptors to this day. "I wrote my master's thesis on cork sensory quality control," he says. "I came up with a protocol to statistically evaluate cork taint. I wrote a manual and it was published, which was kind of cool. It made it to Amazon, where its popularity was in the two millions." The trip to France included a tour of great wineries in Burgundy and Champagne; a classmate of his was at Moët.

"Long story short, I got a great education," he says. "But then it was time to get a job." He turned back to Sichel, who knew the owner of Franciscan, a Napa estate. Suprenant worked there in 1996 and '97 running quality control in the lab. Then his father got ill, and he got the urge to come home. In the meantime, his father was setting up a trip to Long Island for members of the International Wine & Food

Society. "You know how fathers brag about their sons," he says. "He talked to Jerry Gristina, who just happened to be looking for a winemaker."

The Gristinas owned the property on the Main Road in Cutchogue that is now operated by Macari. In between, the winery was bought by Vincent Galluccio in 2000 in a record sale at the time for $5.5 million. Suprenant started in March of 1998. "I'd come back full circle," he says. "But with considerably more knowledge and experience. My classmates and colleagues in Napa thought I was committing career suicide." But he told them to look at a map. "The East End is one of the most beautiful spots in the country. Our lives aren't just about wine. It's about family and being connected to your roots."

During his years at Gristina, Suprenant met Tom Stevenson, who had started at Davis just when he was leaving. Stevenson was the vineyard manager, and it was the start of a lasting relationship. When Galluccio took over, Suprenant and he "disagreed on a philosophical basis."

"He wanted to go from zero to 60 and be the biggest without focusing on quality. He wanted to use all the gimmicks." As a result, Suprenant was soon out of a job. But Stevenson had moved on to Osprey's Dominion. "He recruited me," he says, and started as the winemaker in 2004.

The first order of business was to replant. "The original vineyards were virused," he says. "There was too much pinot noir, and almost 30 acres out of the 70 were chardonnay." The vines were replaced with the breadth of varieties listed above. "It gives us a niche," says Suprenant. "Almost everyone makes chardonnay and merlot; it's hard to get attention in the marketplace."

His first vintage—2001, a great growing season—wasn't released until 2005, when the winery won Winery of the Year at the New York Wine & Food Classic, a competition organized by Finger Lakes-based New York Wine and Grape Foundation, which New York vintners take seriously.

In 2008 Suprenant branched off and made his first wine under his own brand, Coffee Pot Cellars. The pot in the name refers to a lighthouse off Greenport, a village on the North Fork. "You only have one chance to make a first impression," he says as he opens a bottle of Coffee Pot's 2008 Merlot. "I want Coffee Pot to be a very focused quality oriented small batch wine portfolio." To make the wine he bought fruit from a vineyard in further west in Aquebogue, on Tuthill's Lane, owned by Sam McCullough, the vineyard manager at Lenz, just down the street, where his old friend Eric Fry works.

McCullough is a little known lynch pin in Long Island wine history. The insiders know him well. Outsiders rarely hear of him.

McCullough has been farming vineyards since the early 1980s. For instance, he had among his charges Southold Vineyard, then owned by Dean Goldin, who was a partner in the live music venue Wild Rose in Bridgehampton, and who owned the Station, a restaurant in Water Mill. Southold Vineyard was selling their fruit to Bridgehampton. He in turn sold it to former pharmaceutical advertising agency entrepreneur Joel Lauber and his young wife Peggy. Lauber had taken a golden parachute when his business was sold to a British concern. They had thought to start a deli or some other small business, when Peggy said, "Why don't we buy a vineyard?"

Joel and Peggy bought the property in 1993 and re-christened it Corey Creek, which is now a part of Bedell after the Laubers sold to Michael Lynne in 1999 and walked away in 2000. Peggy is now national sales director at Wölffer.

McCullough has been doing it that long. His experience and connections are unquestioned.

"He's a real winegrower. He's out there dropping crop and picking only when the grapes are ready. That's what makes him different. And the difference is the terrior," says Suprenant, referring to the French term that accounts for the difference in taste and quality among vineyards; some attribute it to the soil, weather or climate. "My definition of terroir," he says, "includes the people behind the enterprise. If you give five winemakers fruit from the same vineyard, you get five different wines. But all have the same thread, and the quality shows in the bottle.

"This 2008 merlot represents a leap of faith," he says. "When I'm making wine for myself, it's a very personal enterprise. Every winemaker dreams about a wine representing their own efforts."

The year Suprenant chose to get started with his own label was "not a superstar vintage by any means," he says. And even he questioned McCullough's judgment. "I walked into the vineyard in October and saw a little bit of rot coming in and got nervous. 'You want to make good wine, don't you' said Sam. He got another 10 days of hang time." The extra time produced riper fruit but also resulted in a smaller harvest. "He leaves all the rot on the ground when he picks," says Suprenant. "And those 10 days made all the difference."

He sips the wine. "It's six years old and still's got all the structure and elements of the fruit," he says. "It's not young, but doesn't have that dried raisiny character." The greenish basil element, typical of merlot, is integrated, he says, which is one of the things that makes merlot one of Long Island's premiere grapes. It's not overripe and high in alcohol like it can be in hotter regions like California. "It's kind of nice to know," he says. "Do Long Island wines age? I would say the answer is yes, and 10 to 12 years is not unreasonable for a top quality vintage.

"The other unique thing about this wine is that I think it's wine distilled to its essence. It's a single vineyard, single varietal wine, expressing the terroir of Sam's vineyard. There's nowhere to hide. It's a showcase for Long Island's top red, which is merlot."

Suprenant says this as he stands behind the counter of his new tasting room on the Main Road in Cutchogue, which he shares with his wife Laura Klahre, a beekeeper. The shelves hold wine as well as honey and candles and crayons made out of beeswax. "You know, my father ran three movie theaters, and I worked behind the candy counter," he says looking around. "And lo and behold, I'm working behind another candy counter."

a vision of a
SUSTAINABLE
LONG ISLAND

Barbara Shinn, Steve Mudd, Alice Wise and Libby Tarleton: Environmental Balance

Behind the Workbook: *VineBalance*

Much the same way winemakers enter the business of making wine, winegrowers approach it from different directions. Some are born into it, some go to school for it, and some decide to take a leap and learn as they go. The following growers, Barbara Shinn of Shinn Estate Vineyards in Cutchogue, Steve Mudd of Mudd Vineyards in Southold and Alice Wise of Cornell Cooperative Extension of Suffolk County have added to the knowledge needed to grow good grapes on Long Island.

Wise holds a special place; her work as the viticulturist and education specialist at the extension since 1991 has informed decision making in all aspects of local viticulture: from clonal selection to pest protection to disease alleviation and soil amendments. (Wise wants to make sure the term "clone" when used in the context of grape vines does not mean any type of genetic engineering. "Clones are field selections," she says. "They are selected out and then put through a certification program because they have been identified as distinct and differ from existing clones in very subtle ways, in flavor, cluster size and shape." Because grape vines are propagated by cuttings, not seeds, the only way to isolate the vines that grow best in certain regions is to cut off a cane from an existing plant that does well, plant it again and see if it keeps performing. Farmers working with seeds do something similar by saving seeds from their best, say, tomatoes, and planting them again next year.)

Wise started her plant life as a student of ornamental agriculture in her home state's University of Maryland. Her father grew up on a farm that grew a spectrum of foodstuffs, including melons and grain and animals. "I don't know what happened to his farm," she says. "He had five siblings."

While in Maryland, Wise visited Boordy Vineyards, which grows mostly hybrids on a farm northeast of Baltimore, and was impressed with what she saw. "I began to think of that as a potential career," she says, so she wrote up what she calls an ambiguous application for grad school that could have taken her further into ornamentals or down the road of grapes. She ended up at Cornell University in Gevena, N.Y., where she studied in the department of pomology, a branch of botany that studies and cultivates fruit, with a specialization in viticulture.

"There were a bunch of jobs open in fruit trees, like apples," she says. But then she found out about a job at the extension on Long Island. Larry Perrine, a current owner of Channing Daughters in Bridgehampton and a soil scientist by training, was running viticulture research there. He went up to Geneva to interview, "and graciously offered me the job," says Wise. Her first tasks were to study fruit trees and small fruits like strawberries. For one year, Wise left the extension and worked in the industry under the tutelage of Sam McCullough, who at the time was managing a number of vineyards before he settled down full time in 1989 to the job he still holds at the Lenz Winery. "It was a great learning experience," says Wise. "He's a great guy; it was so helpful."

Perrine left to help found Gristina Vineyards and be the winemaker there, and Wise took over as the viticultural researcher in 1991.

"One of the big priorities when I started was learning about plant materials," she says. "Different types of chardonnay were just being recognized." She was able with the trial vineyard on the extension's property to test them and see how they'd perform on Long Island soil with the Long Island climate. When she started, the vineyard was about a half-acre. That was grubbed up and gradually replanted until it reached the 1.7 bearing acres it has today. "There's room for a bit more," she says. Mostly vinifera grapes are going through trials, but she also has a few hybrids. "We take things out that don't perform well and that the industry really isn't interested in and plant new things periodically."

She was also able to facilitate the earliest plantings on Long Island of Dijon clones of chardonnay. Previously, most chardonnay on Long Island had come out of Foundation Plant Services (FPS), a self-supporting service department in the College of Agricultural and Environmental Sciences at the University of California, Davis, which was mostly working with chardonnay cloned in California. In the early 1990s, says Wise, FPS started importing French clones, which have turned out to grow more readily on Long Island. Wise continued research Perrine started on bird netting and ventured into what is today in the vanguard of viticultural practices: sustainable wine growing.

In 2002, Wise wrote a grant that allowed her to hire Libby Tarleton, who was brought on to create a statewide system for low-impact viticulture. In what came to be known as VineBalance, the women set up workbooks, check sheets and action plans that would balance the needs for protecting the water supply, the soil, business viability and the health of workers. VineBalance came to be template for Long Island Sustainable Winegrowing, a self-regulating group with third-party oversight that started in 2012 with four founders. Today there are 18 members.

And Wise and Tarleton keep studying ways to improve fruit quality. The latest innovation they're testing is a proprietary organic nutrient that, when sprayed on a vine's leaves, will elongate the stem of the grape cluster, known as the *rachis,* thereby putting space between the grapes on a plant known for tight clusters rendering them less susceptible to rot, a no-joke problem on Long Island where humidity doesn't just affect humans.

In the meantime she communicates with all growers via contributions to a weekly newsletter, the Long Island Fruit and Vegetable Update, from April through September and writes six articles per year for the monthly publication *Suffolk County Agricultural News.* She also is the administrator of an industry-only listserv. She and Tarleton also visit farms to discuss vineyard management and host and occasionally speak at grower meetings.

One milestone she notes in the region's history is the 1988 symposium organized by Larry Perrine, Maritime Climate Winegrowing: Bringing Bordeaux to Long Island. "That was a huge step forward."

For the future, Wise and Tarleton expect to continue to help LISW evolve, and assimilate the know-how of veteran growers into her work. "There are a lot of knowledgeable people," she says, "vineyard managers who work seven days a week for months of the year. Steve Mudd helped plant half of the industry. His breadth of knowledge and experience is very helpful to new people, myself included."

Steve Mudd would laugh at this. As wry and voluble as Wise carefully chooses her words, he'll be the first to say, "No one makes more mistakes than us. How do you know what to do until you go out and screw it up?" Mudd's recall of names and dates would make for an interesting evening, once the wine is flowing. But it's the stories about the people who had a hand in creating Long Island Wine Country that will keep you past midnight laughing and having a good time.

Here's one before we start. "Have you heard of the Heublein Auction," he asks. "It's a famous auction in Chicago where they auction off old wines. You know, Petrus, all those really old wines. I'm guessing it was '78, '79, and Chuck Mara, who was from Rochester and owned a couple of big liquor stores, bought the most expensive bottle of wine—I don't remember what it was—for $50,000. I knew these guys, because they'd fly into Mattituck with the winemaker who owned the Syracuse Stainless Steel Tank Company, look around for the afternoon, and fly home. I asked him: How can you justify spending that much? He said, 'I get my name in the paper every day from being this crazy guy who spent $50,000 on a bottle of wine. All over the world. I couldn't buy that much publicity.' So he goes back home and puts the bottle in the window of his wine shop where everyone can see it and marvel at the fool who spent so much. Then one day he put the bottle up as part of a fundraiser and everyone who bought tickets could have a sip of the wine. The night of the event, he tripped and fell and broke the bottle of wine! He got even bigger press for that. So I asked him: 'It was bad, wasn't it?' Of course it was, it had spent time cooking in the window of a store."

Steve Mudd was meant to be in the airplane business like his father, David, who was a pilot, a pilot who married one of the singing McGuire Sisters and who planted peaches, hay and grain on his farm in Southold on the North Fork, where Mudd spent the bulk of his childhood. The hay they brought to a racetrack, Parr Meadows, which used to be in Yaphank, further west up the island, off the Long Island Expressway. "We'd take bales to the stables on race days to feed the horses," he says. They also had a profitable contract with a kosher bakery, to which they sold wheat and rye. "The rabbi would come out when we were planting and visit a few times a year," he says. "And then we had to have the greens to the bakery before sundown on the day of harvest."

Come around 1973, when the Hargraves first planted vinifera grapes to make wine, Mudd was 20 years old and fresh out of job in aerospace technology in Miami due to the energy crisis, when Americans could only buy gas every other day depending on the last number on their licenses plates, odd or even. "My dad was sending me articles about the Hargraves, which said there were beatniks coming to Long Island," he says. "They were pretty comical, but my dad was interested. We got some plants on their order and in 1974 planted one acre on the south side of the road—it's now County Road 48—of sauvignon blanc, pinot noir, gewürztraminer, chardonnay, cabernet sauvignon and merlot." That acre has since been ripped out, and the Mudd's farmstead was demolished when the road was built. They planted again in 1975 on the north side of the road on the home farm's 32 acres, this time putting in four acres of cabernet sauvignon, two acres of pinot noir and one acre of sauvignon blanc. "We plowed, put plastic on top like you do for strawberries and just stuck a cutting into the ground; they're still there today." The unorthodoxy of it was that they didn't graft the vines onto rootstock impervious to phylloxera, a mite that devastated European vineyards in the mid-19th century. Since then, grafting vinifera vines onto American rootstock has been a matter of course when planting a vineyard. "We had the great Dr. Nelson Shaulis, who was the director of viticulture for Cornell and developed the Geneva double curtain [a vine training system], make numerous trip down here, each time telling us it wouldn't work." But it has.

"I'm of the mindset that it's not necessary to graft vines. There are as many disadvantages as there are advantages," says Mudd. "A vine has 50 percent less of a chance of getting a virus on its own roots. Vine certification is not perfect. It's always been a problem making sure you have clean material."

Mudd can also tell the story that the Hargraves were the first to plant vinifera vines on Long Island for wine. The first to plant them—for table grapes—was John Wickham, whose orchard and farm stand still operate in Cutchogue. It wasn't a big business; Vinifera grapes are small, full of seeds and most have thick skins. "But I'd rather eat those grapes than the ones you get in the supermarket," says Mudd. "Most people don't realize how sweet they are." Birds do, however. The birds really do.

"I don't know why anyone came up with the term 'bird brain,'" he says. "They're brilliant; they steal all their fruit for a living." This is why bird netting is so important on Long Island and was and continues to be a focus for the researchers at the extension. "There's nothing anyone likes better than wine grapes," says Mudd. "It's easier to name the birds that don't eat grapes than the ones that do. Robins are the absolute worst. They're smart and they're devastating. The problem is, they don't eat grapes, they bust them up, and then you've got open-wire fermentation, and when you walk through the vineyard, you smell vinegar. It's quite disheartening." Mudd would rather they took a whole grape up into a tree. If he could, he'd plant five acres in the middle of every vineyard just for they birds. "They could have it," he says.

These problems weren't on the minds of the men and women who decided to plant grapes out here in the mid-1980s, says Mudd. At that time tax incentives gave back two dollars for every dollar invested, and land values were going up 25 percent per year. "That's the reason we have wine out here," he says. "And that's why I don't seeing the region getting much bigger. But I could be wrong." But he does see it as being here to stay. His son, Steve, 28, has followed him into the business, and plans to keep it the way it is. The Mudds have never made their own wine. "You'd need six heads for all the hats you're going to wear," he says.

For now, he'll continue managing 12 vineyards and consulting with three more. And working toward the sustainability standards initiated by Alice Wise.

Wise's workbook, *VineBalance,* was written for the entirety of New York State. In 2011, four vineyard managers on Long Island decided to take it on themselves and adapt it for their businesses; along the way, they created guidelines for a way of farming that has the least impact on the soil and water while enhancing the economics and human capital of growing wine. The result was Long Island Sustainable Winegrowing (LISW). Barbara Shinn—along with Larry Perrine of Channing Daughters, Richard Olsen-Harbich of Bedell Cellars and Jim Thompson of Martha Clara in Riverhead—was one of the founders.

Shinn, along with husband David Page, who serves as winemaker at Shinn Estate Vineyard with Patrick Caserta, is a refugee from the restaurant business in New York City, where she and Page owned Home in Greenwich Village. Home was one of the first farm-to-table restaurants; it opened in 1993 and made a name for itself by focusing on local products and making its own ketchup. Page grew up in a farming family in Wisconsin, where his mother's parents grew everything they ate. "His grandfather was quite the hunter," says Shinn, "and David grew up driving combines." By 1997, Shinn says the couple knew the restaurant business wasn't going to last forever, so they started looking around and fell in love with the North Fork. They quickly bought their farm, with the full intention of planting a vineyard, on Oregon Road in Cutchogue, a long stretch that still is home to potato farms, including Martin Sidor's, next store, who has found new customers making potato chips.

In 2000, Shinn and Page started planting Bordeaux reds—merlot, cabernet sauvignon, cabernet franc and malbec—which eventually covered 20 acres of the 22-acre property. The remaining acres house their winery and bed-and-breakfast.

"David and I plotted out the vineyard ourselves," says Shinn. "We never used any consultants and just started reading about everything." They researched rootstocks to see what would grow well in their gravelly loam soil and asked a lot of questions. Shinn credits Wise and Napa nursery owner John Caldwell as great resources.

"Going back to Home restaurant," says Shinn, "we were always working with farmers and teaching our staff what sustainable food was. That's the way David always cooked and it evolved into the way we've been growing wine here." She continues: "Since we weren't professional growers and new, we were able to ask questions. Can we use natural fertilizers? Can we not use weed killers? Are weeds really bad for vines, which are woody? Maybe weeds are beneficial, and we need competition on the vineyard floor. We were enthusiasts from the start and comfortable using experimentation."

In 2004 and 2005 Shinn converted her vineyard floor to a meadow of native vegetation.

"We started mowing under the trellises to control weeds instead of using weed killers or mechanical hoes," she says. "This was brand new; it had never been done anywhere on the East Coast. When the natural vegetation really started to evolve by 2006 and 2007, we saw a dramatic decrease in problematic insects in our vineyard. We had created a beneficial bug habitat; the beneficial insects would eat the problematic insects." Now she has a preponderance of praying mantis, lady bugs and parasitic wasps, "the little ones, not the scary ones," that eat the smaller bugs and mites that are really damaging to wine grapes.

Shinn also turned to nature for the soil. "I feed my living soil with compost, seaweed, fish, whey from the local dairy, diluted sea water and peanut shells," she says. "And by 2006, 2007, we started seeing a much better balance in the vines. They were not growing as aggressively. The vines were a bit smaller but still flowering at the same time as everyone else's."

"This is a very disciplined method of farming," says Shinn. "It's a lot about not interrupting the natural cycles, so nature will balance herself. It's very hands off; we allow the outside ecosystem to come into the vineyard."

There are some things beyond the ability of nature to balance when growing grapes. "I have found it impossible to control downy mildew by using sustainable methods. I cannot be economically viable losing that much fruit," says Shinn. "I use EPA-rated low impact materials that other sustainable programs similar to ours use." The vineyard is not certified organic, which is fine, says Shinn, because in order to be so, one must use 100 percent organic materials. "We're part of the sustainable winegrowers."

LISW's standards came into effect in 2012. "It's not just a workbook," says Shinn. "It's really an exacting protocol. We have materials we don't allow at all: a few insecticides, especially neonicotinoids, which are especially harmful to bees. We limit the amount of synthetic nitrogen and any fungicide that shows in ground water." Long Island gets its drinking water solely from aquifers that sit under the farms, houses and roadways.

"We have to have biological set asides that allow biodiversity and gives habitat to beneficial insects," she says. "We also use integrated pest management; we have to scout the vineyard for problem insects and document in written form what we used and how we used it."

These records are reviewed by a third party that has to pass ethical conventions used by other sustainable growers in the United States and is paid by member dues. "That person wants to read it," says Shinn, "and he can't have any conflict of interest."

Part of the protocol is to create an action plan and review it at the end of the year. "You can then see if you addressed each item," says Shinn, "and see if you're successful in making a better farm growing environment for yourself and your workers."

When she implemented the practices, Shinn says she was surprised how much it helped her accomplish things because she had it in writing. "I saw we had some erosion in a tractor path, and I wanted to reseed it," she says. "Or then it gets out of control and the rains come and then the gullies and washing and then it's five times as hard to fix." She also wrote that she was going to give a composting workshop to other members of the group, and in the winter of 2014, she did.

And importantly there is more and more collaboration. By mid-2014 there were 18 members of LISW: the original four plus

Wölffer Estate, Kontokosta Winery, Corwith, Roanoke, Mudd, Harbes, One Woman, Surrey Lane, Sparkling Pointe, McCall, Palmer, Lieb Cellars, Sannino Bella Vita and Mattebella. "This winter, it was so cold," says Shinn. "And we were on the phone talking about what to do, leave extra canes on in case we need them? And asking 'Are you seeing what I'm seeing?'"

Shinn sees nothing but progress on the horizon. "This region has so much momentum with sustainable growing," she says. "If we stay on this track, this region could have some of the healthiest soils in the country. All of the regions on the East Coast are looking to adopt these practices. And, we're making better wine because of it."

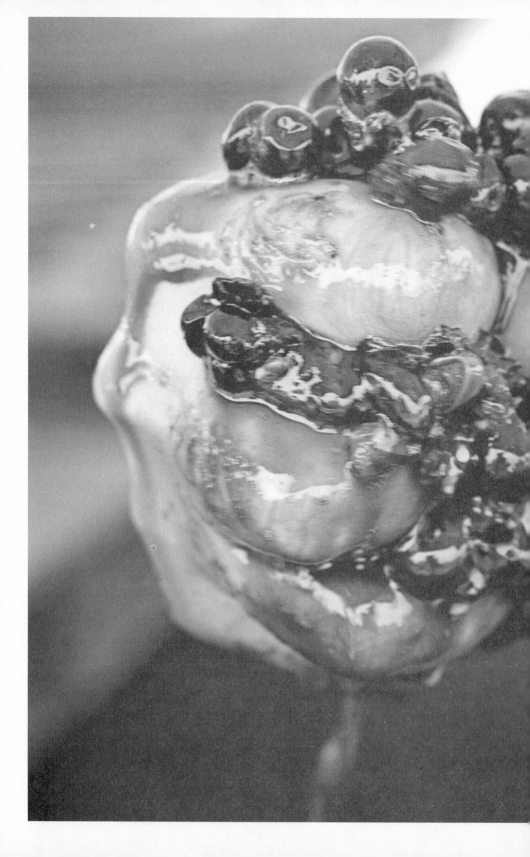

Larry Perrine and James Christopher Tracy: Innovation by the Bottle

Behind the Bottles:
Channing Daughters 2012 Lagrein;
2007 and 2012 Vino Bianco

The two men behind the winemaking at Channing Daughters in Bridgehampton on the East End's South Fork are born-and-bred Californians. James Christopher Tracy grew up in the Bay Area, studied philosophy and the performing arts before ending up in cooking school in New York. Larry Perrine grew up in Southern California, in Whittier—the home of Richard Nixon's father's grocery, he points out—studied English, went back to school to study soil science, and ended up as a grad student at Cornell during the fledgling years of Finger Lakes wine country.

The two met in 2000 at Channing Daughters when Perrine was the winemaker and Tracy and his wife, Allison Dubin, were members of the wine club. "Chris asked me why we weren't making a chardonnay using indigenous yeast in a barrel," says Perrine. "I said, 'Here's your juice and barrel, knock yourself out.' Within a year he was working for us. And it was fantastic."

"There are some people who plan their lives," says Perrine. "I never done that; I go for the most interesting thing. You could say I'm not totally practical."

Looking at how Channing makes its wine, it's hard to disagree with his self-assessment. All the wines are small batch, which winemakers agree makes for a lot of extra work. Channing doesn't just make one rosé, in 2013 they made seven; at any one time they could have 14 whites, four orange wines and 11 reds on offer. When they decided to go into vermouth, they didn't make a red and a white, they made five, using botanicals sourced from within a few miles of the winery. All the wines are based on fruit either from the home vineyard, where 25 acres are planted in traditional varietals but also in grapes indigenous to the northeastern parts of Italy, including pinot grigio, tocai friulano, refosco, franconia (also known as blaufränkish), malvasia bianca, teroldego, lagrein and dornfelder. When they decided to make a ripasso—an Italian technique where one wine is refermented along with new grape juice—they threw in a twist by reserving half the finished wine to pass over the next year's vintage. They're now up to Variation 6 for the vermouth. Some wines they make by vinifying all the blending elements separately. Some they make by picking all the blending elements at the same time and then vinifying them together, which is called a field blend. Must I go on? I can, because I haven't told you how to make orange wines, which involves white grapes that go through fermentation with their skins in the mix; Channing does this in open tanks, oak barrels and bins, or "bucketed out and pressed off then put in 78 percent new oak and 22 percent two-year-old oak where the wine spent 20 months before it was bottled by gravity." (Quote from their website.) It is a momentous job to keep track of all this, which Tracy does mostly by keeping his head down and letting the wine speak for him. But when asked to speak about his wine in front of crowds and at functions highlighting Long Island wine, as he often is, he is as outspoken as he is closed mouthed about his history and personal life. He can rattle off facts about winemaking and the history of winemaking that demonstrate how much of a student of wine he is. He has written about his work in a column in *Edible East End* magazine, where you could learn all about his "Winemaker Wonderings." But don't expect to learn about anything that happens off the vineyard or out of the winery.

Perrine, however, is a natural storyteller with a rich background and a recall for fun facts—such as that grocery store—and the mechanics of pH in in winegrowing. Where Tracy's interests are above ground, Perrine's mostly lay in the soil where legumes symbiotically fix nitrogen levels with the cooperation of a bacteria that infects their roots. He can also tell you the differences among Riverhead loam, Haven loam and Bridgehampton loam and how they impact the wine grown in them. His e-mail address isn't theguru@channingdaughters.com for nothing. So we'll delve into his history, which involves women, wine, and a lot of time in school.

Besides the grocery store, Whitter is also the final home of Pio Pico, the last governor of Mexican California, who died in 1894, Perrine will have you know. Perrine, the first person in his family to go to college, was raised by his father, a worker in the aerospace industry, who himself was raised in Colorado, where his family lost its farm in the Dust Bowl.

"My mother's from Utah," he says, "grew up on the slopes of a copper mine, which ate the mountain away. I've visited there many times; I'm a westerner." His parents met in the aviation industry at the beginning of World War II. "My dad got drafted and my mother got pregnant with my brother, who was born in 1945." He adds, "I was born in 1951 after the war, definitely part of the baby boomers."

In high school, he was not a science geek, and had one foot in the jock world and "another in the intellectual world as the editor of the campus newspaper."

After high school, Perrine says he was kind of an itinerant student, with time spent in Utah and in the California system, where he finished his degree in English at Cal State Fullerton. "I then started a relationship with a professor and moved in with her in Laguna Beach," he says. "Life was never the same. I had to become an adult, instead of becoming an adult with juvenile friends, who were more interested in Quaaludes."

Perrine was quickly swept into the social life of the English faculty. "I spent the last year and a half of school going to dinner parties with these same people, many of whom became friends," he says. "It was of its time. This was the early '70s, and the older faculty didn't think much of it."

Soon he was visiting Europe and drinking wine, "not flavored wine." The two eventually got married and started to travel in California wine country. "Mondavi opened in 1966," he says. "There were only six wineries then." He starts to tick them off: Mondavi, Martini, Inglenook, Christian Brothers, Charles Krug. "OK, maybe there were five." By the early '70s that changed, several new wineries started going up, and Perrine spent more time in Europe, where he learned to love wine. "But I didn't know what to do," he says. "I had a degree in English and the Baby Boom had crested. They were laying off teachers. My high school closed in 1977. It's now a college of chiropractic."

Wouldn't you know, his next job was in a liquor store, in beautiful Laguna Beach, where he became the wine specialist. "No one else knew about it," he says. In the meantime he started a garden. "We were hippies, it was back to the land,

and I thought this is so much fun, so exciting. Maybe someone should pay me to do this." The next step was to investigate agricultural colleges, and Laguna Beach was near two. He visited Cal Poly in Pamona, where there's a focus on technical education, and met with different departments. "I finally found the right people when I talked to the soil scientists," he says. "It was agronomy; that's for the kids going back to the farms."

So he returned to school as an undergrad and had to take the science and math he missed the first time around. "It was really hard," he says. "And by now I'm 23 years old and the rest of the kids are 18. I became the student I couldn't have been at any other time. I had discovered what I loved: plants, plant science, microbiology, plant nutrition—soil science."

"All my professors wanted me to go to grad school where they went," he says—and this introduced his next decision. "Advanced academics was a pathway." So he considered Cornell, UC Davis and the University of Minnesota. "I didn't really want to stay in California," he says. "It's so flat and hot in Davis." Cornell seemed far away, but Minnesota had the only urban farm campus in the United States. "I was tuned in to feed the world," says Perrine. "There were famines in Africa. Fish farming became avant guard. There was the *Mother Earth News*."

St. Paul, where the university is based, was exciting, says Perrine. "I had a wonderful five years there. It was a beautiful place, and I got real world farm experience for a suburban kid." He learned how to drive a tractor and how *not* to drive a tractor. "We worked with sugar beets, wheat; I had become a scientist." For Perrine it was like coming full circle to his father's farming roots. "He was charmed by the idea," he says. "My parents did not have a vision for me, or expectations for me; they were glad I was happy, and hoped I'd get a job someday." After school, he spent the next three years working in food co-ops and politics. The international guys he met told him his ideas were noble, "but it's not about production, it's about politics. It's politics and corruption that keep people hungry." So he became interested in food policy. "Talk about the counter culture," he says. "It was a profoundly interesting time." But it was also decision time. "I could eventually run political campaigns successfully and stay there, or I could go back and work with plants."

It was 1979 and he saw a front-page article in the *New York Times* about the Finger Lakes. "The vinifera revolution was just beginning to take root," he says. "I didn't really want to go home and work in Napa, where there were plenty of jobs for people like me." Not being a practical one, he decided to visit the Finger Lakes, because his first wife was from Troy, N.Y. "I made a wild-ass leap, sold my house in Minneapolis and arrived in the Finger Lakes in 1980." He went to a now-defunct winery on Kekua Lake, where he worked for a year and a half. "The oenologist recruited me to go back to grad school at Cornell," he says, which was his entrée to Long Island.

Cornell is a land grant school that operates extensions all over the state of New York that do agricultural research. And at that time, several growers on Long Island had put some money up for a research station on Long Island and wanted to hire a grad student.

"I did my first technical work on Long Island from 1983 to '85," he says. The few wineries and vineyards in operation had some growing problems. "And—serendipity—that was my specialty." Perrine determined the soil on Long Island was acidic. "That was fine for potatoes, but when they started growing grapes the recommendation was not to add lime because it would encourage growth. That was the first phase," he says. "But people had to continue to lime because rainfall is naturally acidic, and you have to maintain balance or you'll introduce nutrient disorders."

Perrine moved to Long Island in 1985 to work for Dave Mudd, (father of our friend Steve) the original wine-country vineyardist. After a year, Suffolk County, with Cornell, created a research position at the extension in Riverhead. "I was a full-time researcher for wine grapes," he says. "We worked on bird control. And now, with the help of the growers and animal damage specialists at Cornell, bird netting is completely universal."

Of all the pests affecting winegrowing on Long Island, bird pressure is the worst, although the deer are pretty bad, too. The East End lies directly under a migratory path, and a mass migration starts just when the grapes begin to ripen. It's no surprise that ripe grapes are like crack to birds, especially the starlings. Perrine worked at Cornell for three years, when, in 1988 Jerry Gristina contacted him. "It was an opportunity the start a new winery from scratch," says Perrine. "We built the out buildings and made wine." He spent seven years there, before starting a consulting career for vineyard operations nationwide.

He also went into a consulting business, called Wine Works, with Richard Olsen-Harbich, who was, at the time, fresh off his job at Bridgehampton Winery. "I traveled a lot," says Perrine. "It was an interesting time."

In the meantime, he had moved on in his personal life. "I was no longer married to my first wife," he says. "I moved to Sag Harbor in 1994, where I've been ever since. Then I got a call from Palmer's winemaker Tom Drozd, who told me he knew a guy not far from Sag Harbor who needed help.

"In the summer of 1995, I met Walter Channing," he says, "and it was true, he needed help; he had gotten in a little over his head." Channing had planted 13 acres of grapes on his property on Scuttlehole Road in Bridgehampton. "Which is a lot," says Perrine. "One acre is a lot of plants to take care of." The two decided to go into the wine business together. "He put more money into it than I did, so he got to name it. We made our first wine at Peconic Bay Winery [which was then owned by Ray Blum], in 1996, and in '97, we made our wine here. In this building." The winery and tasting room opened to the public in summer 1998; by 1999 they had planted 10 more acres, mostly Italianate varietals. In 2000, he met Chris Tracy, who with his wife, was approximately the 15th couple to sign up for the Channing wine club. Club members were invited to meet once a month and go through the whole process of making wine. "It was a good bonding experience," says Perrine. Tracy decided to leave his sous chef job in the city and move out to work in a restaurant in the Hamptons to be closer to the winery. "Chris's family owned a vineyard in the Spring Mountain district in

Napa," says Perrine. "He had been drinking wine since he was young and had traveled to European wine regions. Next thing I knew he's hanging around harvest." And then Tracy popped the "indigenous yeast" question. The first wines were like an engagement ring. Pretty soon they were married.

Tracy's restaurant job didn't work out, so Perrine took a leap of faith and asked him to come to the East End anyway. "I told him we'd work it out," says Perrine. "I couldn't afford not to. This is a talent that just showed up on my doorstep, a highly driven talent. So Walter and I made them [Tracy and his wife, Allison] partners years ago. So they have a piece of the action and a lot of the responsibility. I told Allison, 'You like this, right? Well get ready, 10 years will go by in the blink of an eye." Perrine married again to a former restaurateur after his second wife died; she works at Channing as well.

It's been 13 years since Tracy started, and Channing Daughters has forged a reputation as the place to go for wine geeks and burgeoning wine geeks. The leafy land around the winery is filled with enormous sculptures by Walter Channing, like the upside-down tree or the wooden mask on some of the wine labels. The airy tasting room is lined with all the wines they make; friends come in to drop off eggs from their chickens just as often as someone comes in to buy wine. They don't host many events, and if they do, they're mostly their own.

The focus is on the wine.

Wines such as the 2012 Lagrein and the 2007 and 2012 Vino Bianco, which Tracy and Perrine opened for me in the spring of 2014. The first Vino Bianco, made in 2001 (a good

year on Long Island), was a blend of chardonnay, sauvignon
blanc and pinot grigio; the following year tocai friulano was
added, and it's been that way ever since. The different lots are
vinified separately and made into "a symphonic white blend,"
says Tracy. "This was probably the first white blend made on
Long Island. We think it expresses our terrior really well." One
sniff of the 2007 blows Tracy away. "You see how well it ages,"
he asks, looking over to his mentor for affirmation. "It's aging
like a Burgundy. I'm amazed how much freshness there still is,
even though it's clearly developing."

The wine was turning a slight amber color around the
edges, evidence of its years in bottle, and displaying the kind
of nuttiness you get in older white Burgundies. "I thought it
would be fun to show you," says Tracy. "We have several styles
that develop really well." Tracy held back some of the 2007,
which was a great year for wine grapes, and it's being poured by
the glass in Manhattan. The development shows in the mouthfeel, aromas and flavor. The bright fresh apple fruit it had when
it was younger is now more like baked apple, and is balanced
by the mellowed grapefruitiness of the sauvignon. The addition of the tocai and pinot grigio reflects Perrine's interests in
Italian grape varieties. Planting them was part of a "deliberate
move," Perrine says. "It's sort of transformative, and it has a history." He tells of Lou Iacucci, the owner of Goldstar Wines and
Spirits in Forest Hills, N.Y., who introduced Italian wines to
New Yorkers in the early 1980s and died after a car accident in
Italy in 1988. "He was a pioneer," says Perrine. "He was selling
me these wines, and as a researcher at Cornell I could see how

these varieties would perform here, because I knew what the climate in Friuli was like."

Tracy, stilled wowed by the '07 Vino Bianco, compares it to another bottle of the same vintage he had opened the day before, which had not aged as much. "They're so different," he says. "Which is even more shocking to me. Right? Especially under natural cork. That's crazy. Every bottle has its own life, and these came out of the same case."

The 2012 Vino Bianco, which was made in an above average year, has all the fresh apple, citrus and mild oaky notes you'd expect in a young wine. It fills the mouth and lasts long on the palate with zesty acidity; you know this will help the wine age as long as the 2007.

The 2012 Lagrein was made from one of those Italian varieties. Channing has been making it since 2009 after being the first to plant lagrein on Long Island 2007, and it is right for the site. (Newcomer Regan Meador has put three acres of his new vineyard on the North Fork under lagrein.) The South Fork is a little cooler than the North Fork, where bud break can occur almost two weeks earlier. It's a dusty red wine with an extremely pronounced herbal, barnyard aroma that belies the dark fruitiness in the mouth.

"I'm not frustrated by it," says Perrine, "but I'm curious as to why individuals and the media want to identify a region by a grape varietal. We don't feel compelled to do that; we're compelled to do the opposite. If we look at Friuli for inspiration, that's one of the most diverse regions; they have dozens of white varieties and 10 of the best red wine producers."

Tracy sips the lagrein again. "It's got wild fruit character, with this zingy slightly green tone. They all have it," he says referring to the two previous vintages made in 2009 and 2010. He starts to speak faster. "And the '09, it's still a baby. We're showing them too young. But those wines sing with complexity and sense of place. The flavors, the textures. It's certainly got the stuffing to last, the phenolic content, the tannins."

"It's a high-acid variety," says Perrine. "Just like in the Alto Adige. It is crisp, got a chunky texture. It works when it's young with fatty food."

"Like stinco," interjects Tracy, mentioning the Italian dish of braised pork shank. "That's great with lagrein."

"The varietal is pretty consistent," says Perrine." We could have picked almost any wine to show you. We thought these would be two good examples of transformation for us and Long Island." He adds, "Much of what we've set out to do we've accomplished, even though we didn't have a master plan."

Ron Goerler Jr.: "Wine Is About Time"

Behind the Bottles: Jamesport Vineyards 1997 Merlot and 2001 Cabernet Franc

Each winter, until 2009, the eaves of the barn that houses the tasting room and the winery at Jamesport Vineyards supported colossal icicles. The building was not insulated, so the constant push and pull of the heat generated by the activity inside and the freezing temperatures typical of the dead of winter on the North Fork of Long Island repeatedly thawed and froze its mantle of snow.

The barn has been in the Goerler family since 1986 when the patriarch, Ron Sr., bought it at an auction after the business it housed, the North Fork Winery, which was also a nursery for grape vines, went belly up. Before that, the barn belonged to the family of Tom Drozd, who still works as a winemaker on Long Island, and before that to an old farming family, who left their mark—a carving bearing the year 1901—on a ceiling beam.

In 1986, Ron Goerler Jr. was 20 years old. After a short career as a college student studying soil science—"That didn't work out."—he decided grape farming was his future. "I knew I wanted to work outside," he says.

By that time he knew of what he spoke. He father had bought an apple orchard in Cutchogue five years earlier and planted chardonnay the following year. The family of eight became "weekend warriors," packing the car with the dogs and kids and racing out from Oyster Bay, a town about 60 miles and one hour west, to take care of the vines.

"We did it every weekend," says Goerler. "It was fun. It was exciting. It was like the Wild West, and we were the pioneers."

Pioneers with an unusual pedigree. Ron Sr. ran a successful plumbing supply manufacturing business and also bought and sold horses for trotting races. But when he heard of what he believed would be a renaissance of farming on Long Island, catalyzed by the 1973 planting of vinifera grapes by Alex and Louisa Hargrave just down the road, he started looking to buy some land on the North Fork, where he had vacationed since childhood.

"My dad's a renaissance man," says Goerler. "Always looking into the future, and he's a gambler. He gambled on buying a farm and that it was going to turn out well."

In 1981, it was a gamble. A recession in 1982 and '83 would drive interest rates up to 19 percent and the potato business took a beating; many old farming families had to sell. "I can't believe how many auctions we went to where we saw grown men cry," says Goerler. "All the old names and the Polish families, who had worked here for generations."

So the Goerlers joined a new set of families: the Damianos, who started Pindar; the Mudds, who became the go-to family for those looking to plant vineyards; and the Bedells, whose namesake winery is still one of the first mentioned when discussing Long Island wine.

"When we planted in '82," says Goerler, "the ground was frozen like a brick. I remember Dave Thomas [who now manages the vineyard at Bedell] banging those posts 200 times to get them in the ground; now you can do it with two, with the new machinery. I can still hear it."

It's the sound of history, hard work and money. In those days, says Goerler, it cost $2,500 to plant an acre of grapes. It now costs $200,000. Sure, you're getting better quality vines with more suitable rootstocks, but everyone plants more densely now, uses lasers to keep the rows straight and installs drip irrigation. And you know what you're buying. "A lot of the chardonnay we planted turned out to be pinot blanc," says Goerler. "The nursery supplying everyone couldn't keep up with demand, so they started supplementing with pinot blanc. We always wondered why certain plants would rot before the others."

And costs are crucial to a family that wants to keep the business going. "Farming is a generational thing," says Goerler. "You have to make it to the next generation to make it successful. It's all about time." From the beginning, his father, whose family's roots are in Baden Baden, Germany, was fascinated about the costs of a bottle of wine and getting people to appreciate that. "He always said, 'If you don't understand the cost of it, you're in the wrong business.' A lot of energy goes into that packaging and what it tastes like," says Georler. "He taught me that, and that you have to recoup the money."

The balance between cost and payoff was challenged again in 1985 when Hurricane Gloria stormed across Long Island. "It flattened vineyards out here," says Goerler, who remembers the families pitching into help dig new posts and right the rows plowed down by the wind and the rain after the category 2 storm hit on September 27. "I also remember all the 'Gloria Red' that year," he adds, referring to a lot of wine made from diluted and under ripe red grapes. "You're gambling from the time you start pruning to the time you harvest. You've got a 10-month cycle to make that barrel of wine."

By 1988 Goerler had moved out to the North Fork full time, and by 1990 he met the local girl he would marry, Joanne Zuhoskie, whose family once owned the cauliflower farm the Hargraves bought to start their vineyard. "It was the only way to be accepted out here, to marry into it," says Goerler. He threw himself into managing the vineyard.

In the beginning the family exclusively sold grapes, but realized it was not the best way to make money. Soon they were making wine with Dan Kleck, who left Long Island in 1998 to become the production winemaker at Kendall-Jackson in California and now lives and works in Paso Robles. "I learned a lot from Dan Kleck," says Goerler. "He showed me how to taste wine. His palate was great. He was the one guy I've met who could taste and tell you the wine *and* vintage."

Kleck was the first in a long line of winemakers at Jamesport. "He didn't last with my father," says Goerler. He was followed by Russ Turner, who came from Niebaum Coppola in Napa, where he had great success with Rubicon. He didn't last long either. Sean Capiaux, now winemaker at O'Shaughnessy in Napa and for his own label, Capiaux Cellars, also spent a few years in Jamesport's cellars while his wife attended Cornell. "From Sean I learned about balance," says Goerler. "How to get it, where it comes from and how to handle it in the winery." Other winemakers still in the region moved through also: Russell Hearn and Richard Olsen-Harbich. When Capiaux returned to California, a local man, Les Howard, who had grown up in the business, took over the winemaking. He left for Pindar in 2008, and Goerler assumed the role. Since then he's been the winemaker, vineyard manager, head of the tasting room and sales and marketing.

"For a long time, I couldn't manage the vineyard and make the wine," he says, "but we soon realized that if we were going to make this work, we'd have to do it ourselves." By "ourselves," Goerler means himself and his father. None of his siblings, nor his wife, works at the winery. And he likes it that way. He likes figuring out how to make the business work and how much wine focuses his mind on time and people. "The people you come across," he says, "they teach you something, good or bad. They have helped build me."

That also includes the customers who come into the winery. Sitting in his cellar, Goerler can hear their footsteps above on the barn's wooden floor. (He can also hear the phone ring, and ring. "Why doesn't anyone answer it," he pleads.) "I've learned that if you give them balanced wine, it will appeal to most palates."

But making balanced wine on Long Island took a while to figure out. "In the beginning we all planted cabernet sauvignon," says Goerler. "Why not? California was doing it." Cab does not always ripen well on Long Island; it needs a longer growing season than our cool climate can provide. Many also planted pinot noir, as did Jamesport, but in 2013 Goerler ripped it all out. "I put a lot of energy into pinot," says Goerler, "and it never ripened consistently." Even the grapes that do well were planted on rootstock that made the plants put out too many leaves and not enough fruit. Goerler has ripped those out too. "If there's not replanting going on, there's never going to be new growth," he says. "Farming is a fragile thing. It takes input, and if you're not looking how to get it into the next generation's hand, if you're not thinking about the next 40 years, you're going to have an implosion." For Goerler, that transition is already underway, the renovation of the barn, the replanting and an investment in infrastructure, as well as an expansion of the tasting room, is a way to ensure longevity. It will now be up to his children to decide if they're going to take it on when they are old enough.

"I have three daughters and one son," he says. "When I was their age all I wanted to do was ride dirt bikes. It's hard to find young people who want to farm. You have to make it profitable."

Goerler thinks narrowing his focus is one way to do that. "In the early days we wanted to emulate California, but the wines fell apart," he says. "The wines here are delicate, and we have to produce wine in our own style." After his nearly 30 years in a Long Island vineyard, he believes it's time to get down to two or three wines. "Why not," he asks. "California does it. I truly believe sauvignon blanc and cabernet franc are the varieties for this region: the quality, the ageability, how they taste and how long they last, year after year. Much of what we've planted has been more of a challenge than not."

To demonstrate his choice and what he's learned, Goerler opens a bottle of 1997 Merlot and a 2001 Cabernet Franc. Both were good years, and the '97 was made with Capiaux.

"I maybe have five of these left," says Goerler as he lifts out the cork. "I hope it tastes as beautiful as I remember it." As he pours the wine, Goerler marvels at the color. "It's still ruby red," he says, "not bricky." The wine is clean and smells fresh with that chocolaty minty aroma found in good Saint-Émilion, classic merlot. There is still a lot of fruit left and tannins to balance the natural acidity. "I'm amazed tasting this," he says. "There are people who say Long Island wine is not good. This wine was made extremely well." Goerler adds that he chose this wine because he and Capiaux had argued about the blend. In the United States, a wine must have at least 75 percent of a variety to put that name on the label. The other 25 percent is up to the winemaker, who can choose a blend that will take advantage of what else was good that season to enhance the wine. "Sean believed merlot did well with cabernet franc added," he says. "I wanted to add cabernet sauvignon, which we did the following year. He was right. The backbone of making wine is the blend."

Goerler then opens the cab franc. The aroma jumps out of the glass. Cab franc can take on herbaceous notes of bell pepper, which some people like, but in hot years, like 2001, it becomes spicier and filled with dark fruits. This wine, at 12 years old, was showing pronounced secondary aromas of soy sauce and dried cherries. "It's herbaceous, but not green," says Goerler. "The oak is integrated; it's beautiful. When cab franc is done is this style, it shows how pretty it can be." Indeed the wine is outstanding. The nose is so vibrant; each time you go back, another aroma emerges.

"We won best red that year," says Goerler, referring to the Wine and Food Classic held each year by the New York Wine and Grape Foundation, a competition Long Island winemakers take seriously. "It was the first time for Long Island."

Goerler is pleased with the wine and believes it will last for many more years, as will the merlot. "It's well balanced and represents the variety," he adds, "and it's going to get better and better. I firmly believe this is a great grape, and it's something unique to this area. We do it really well. To be able to make this high quality wine will get us to the next generation," he says. And that will justify the money he's been putting back into the business and his decision to grow retail.

"When I get to that point, when my kid's looking at me and he can say I gave him an opportunity and he ran with it, then it all will be worth it. I can say the same of my father. He had a vision and took a gamble to make a statement by producing wines of this caliber. It's not easy." Looking back, Goerler remembers the naysayers who made fun of the "weekend warriors."

"A lot of people said, 'Your wine sucks,'" he says. "But I believe the industry will be here and be strong as we keep up a level of quality."

He listens again to the customers upstairs. "But how do we educate them," he asks. "How do we get them to understand what we do for a living? It's not just coming out here and getting loopy. It takes a lot to get people to slow down out here. I want them to come and relax and realize life doesn't have to be rushed. Wine is about *time*. It's about time in the bottle and making it and sitting down and drinking it."

He pauses and looks at the open bottles in front of him. "I look at these two vintages—the weather, the choices I made—and I'm clear how they went. I can't say that about my breakfast."

the future of
LONG ISLAND
WINE

Kelly Urbanik Koch: Napa Bred; Long Island Bound

Behind the Bottle: Macari Vineyards 2013 Early Wine

Kelly Urbanik Koch, the winemaker at Macari Vineyards since 2010, attended UC Davis because it was close to home. She grew up in St. Helena, smack dab in the middle of Napa Valley. Went to St. Helena High School, played every sport she could, and sometimes helped her Italian grandfather, who also lived in her hometown, make wine in what the family referred to as the Wine Shed.

"He had a hand-cranked de-stemmer and a little basket press in a small garage," she says from her test-tube filled office in Macari's cellar. "He mostly made red wine. We fermented it in garbage cans and punched it down with a wooden puncher thing. And put most of the stuff in carboys until we bottled it later." When it was finally bottled, Urbanik decorated the labels with markers.

That rudimentary equipment is a far cry from the gear just outside her door. The Macaris are known on Long Island for being adventurous early adopters and advocates of biodynamic wine growing. In 2103 they bought the first concrete egg-shaped tanks on Long Island from a company in California. Their inaugural contents are cabernet franc and sauvignon blanc from the highly anticipated 2013 vintage. Dark colored and smooth, the eggs are irresistible to touch, almost like the belly of a pregnant woman. And inside something is indeed growing. The ovoid construction works almost the same way as a Weber kettle grill, trapping the CO_2 produced by fermentation and forcing a cycle of gas that lessens the need for stirring, or punching down, during fermentation. The shape is also said to be harmonious with the principles of biodynamics, a soil enhancing practice the owners, Joe and Alexandra Macari, use in their vineyards. An additional benefit is that concrete allows a slow ingress of air into the wine. Stainless steel does not. Oak barrels do, but they can impart flavors, wanted or unwanted. Plus the eggs are easy to write on with chalk to label the contents, which is cool.

Even though she came from California, Urbanik Koch never considered going into wine. "I didn't think you could be in the wine industry if your family didn't own a winery," she says. "I went to school with kids like that: I figured that's what they do."

But Davis, one of the leading wine education universities in the country, has a way of drawing you in. In her freshman year, she took the Introduction to Wine class. "I really liked it, so I switched my major, which was biology with a specialty in plant science." And so she joined the other lab rats in her dorm, one of whom now works for Genentech. "There are a lot of labs in the Bay Area," she adds.

The new focus brought her back to the days she enjoyed with her grandfather, whose big garden that had, in addition to grapes, walnut trees and enough vegetables to feed the family. "What attracted me to switching my major," she says, "was having a job where I could work outside."

That summer, outside she was, working in a greenhouse on campus that grew celery and tomatoes. The next summer she worked for one of her enology professors, Andy Walker, a researcher on Pierce's disease, a bacterium that lives in the water-conducting system of plants and is spread from plant to plant by sap-feeding insects. In California, the culprit is the glassy-winged sharpshooter.

"He was super inspirational for me," say Urbanik Koch. "I really looked up to him a lot." Which meant spending her time on a five-acre lot planted with rootstocks to test their resistance to the disease.

She took extra time to finish her senior year, because the volleyball schedule conflicted with some of the labs she needed to graduate. But no matter, Walker helped her get a job at Berringer, a Napa behemoth with vineyards all over the valley. Urbanik Koch got her own truck and spent all her time outdoors monitoring vineyards for disease. "It was great," she says. "They allowed me to work part time." And when she finished school and left the job, she left thinking that her future lay as a vineyard manager.

But travel changes you. Urbanik Koch was able to take advantage of a study abroad program sponsored by Davis and soon was traveling around France, visiting Bordeaux, Burgundy and the Loire Valley. "I also applied to all the international internships," she says, landing a spot with Louis Jadot, the Burgundian mega producer. "I was so scared to go so far away from home, so it was good I got to see it ahead of time."

Her job was in the main cellar where most of Jadot's top-of-the-line wines are made. "It was beautiful," she says. "All gravity fed, and it was interesting to see the quality they could get working with so many different wines, all the appellations in Burgundy."

The bulk of her time was spent in the vineyard, where she learned the habits of her French co-workers, who would leave the tractor running during lunch to bill for the extra hours. "They always got caught," she says. "And the next day we had to hoe all day long." Come August, she was able to take a vacation and to visit friends at Geisenheim, the premier wine school in Germany and check out the cellars in Champagne and Austria. But this was 2003, an infamous summer in Europe where it was so hot that the elderly were dying in un-airconditioned apartments in Paris. No doubt it affected the vintage too. Urbanik Koch was called back to Burgundy, because harvest had to start early.

"It was fast," she says. So much so that she missed the meals served in the dorm owned by Jadot and ended up eating peanut butter and jelly sandwiches. And peanut butter is hard to find in France. "That's when I realized I like working in a winery," she says. The end of her tenure was a visit to the Hospices de Beaune, the fund-raiser/celebration Burgundy throws each year to celebrate harvest. People come from all over the world, old bottles are opened and extravagant meals are served. A fine send off after a few months working in a vineyard and winery!

Back in California, Urbanik Koch started working at Bouchaine in Carneros, the southern part of the Napa Valley. It's a big winery that also works as a custom-crush operation, so she had the opportunity to make many different types of wine from fruit all over the valley. But the wanderlust instilled by her time in Europe peeked out and led her to apply for jobs outside of California. One day she responded to an ad looking for an assistant winemaker that didn't state the location.

"I don't remember applying for it," she says. Then she got a phone call from an area code she had never seen. It was from John Irving Levenberg, the winemaker at Bedell Cellars in Cutchogue. "Once I heard the winery was in New York, I didn't remember anything else he said. "Sorry," she said. "I'm really not interested in moving to New York." Levenberg, a California native himself, would be visiting the Bay Area the following week. "What could it hurt," she thought. Levenberg's enthusiasm was infectious. "He seemed so passionate, and I just really got along with him," she says. "I thought, 'Wow, this is so cool. He really believes in this.'"

Levenberg convinced her to visit the winery—her first time on the East Coast. She arrived on April 3, 2006, worked for two weeks and then flew home to drive back with all her stuff. In the meantime, she and Levenberg visited other East End wineries and tasted wine still in barrel, some of which was juice from the infamous 2005 vintage, a year when the growing season was so hot winemakers got giddy about the ripeness of the fruit only to be thrown when it rained for days over Columbus Day weekend. But Urbanik Koch was impressed. "I thought, 'Wow, they make good wine here,'" she says. "Going to Europe changed my whole perspective, I was ready to go."

After working in the large operations of Jadot and Bouchaine, Urbanik Koch was excited about how winemakers were so much more hands-on on Long Island. "There was stuff here I would have never have gotten to do in California," she says. "I learned so much so fast here. If I still lived in California, I don't think I would yet know how to run a bottling line." She adds that the challenge of finding help on Long Island leads one to figure out how to do it themselves.

Two year later, Levenberg was gone and Urbanik Koch took over as head winemaker. "I felt like I was up for the job," she says. "I was a little nervous, but I enjoyed making decisions, because I knew I could make them." Winemaking requires making decisions to which there are no right answers, she adds. "It's kind of doing what you think feels right."

For help with that, she had the winery's founder, Kip Bedell on hand. "If Kip wasn't there, I'm not sure I would have felt the same way," she says. "He was a guiding factor. He never told me what to do. Never said, 'You should do this.' He would let me make the decision, and then speak up if he thought it was a good idea. He was like a father figure to me. Still is."

As it happens in creative fields like wine and cooking, Urbanik Koch moved on in 2010 to be the head winemaker at Macari, where she felt at home right away. "They have a lot of trust in me," she says. "They give me feedback, and the whole family is really involved, which can be difficult, though it's not difficult here."

Her first year was getting to know the 200 acres of vineyards, large for Long Island, working to finish the 2010 wines that had yet to be bottled and learning the legacy of previous winemakers and consulting winemakers, which include Helmut Gangl, an Austrian who created the Macari Early Wine, the wine Urbanik Koch chose to take us behind.

Macari's Early Wine is a great entrée into what the Macari Family and winemaker Kelly Urbanik Koch are all about. It takes tradition, innovation and practicality all into account.

Let's start with the year. The 2013 vintage will be one for the ages, spoken of in the hushed tones formerly reserved for 1993, when beautiful weather blessed then-emerging Long Island Wine Country. 2013 started late, after recovering from a harsh winter and the after effects of Superstorm Sandy. Luckily East End vineyards are not close enough to the coastline to be threatened by flooding, but salt spray and excessive winds gave everyone pause. The growing season slowly warmed with intermittent rain and some heat spikes. Some vineyards experienced flowering trouble, which can reduce yields, but it was site specific. The real ringer came in the fall when the region went 57 days without rain. In a maritime climate where the threat of hurricanes hovers over harvest, this is more than a big deal. The arid weather staved off mildew, mold and rot and allowed the grapes to slowly reach record levels of ripeness. One vineyard manager said she heard of someone getting a second harvest. A fable? Who cares? 2013 deserves it. The dry harvest season also allowed growers to choose when to pick, no hurrying to get the grapes in before a deluge, like what happened in 2005, the year before Urbanik Koch left Napa Valley behind to come to Long Island.

Now consider early wine. Macari's first early wine was created by Gangl in 2003. He wanted to recreate the Jungwein (young wine) of his homeland. Let's not forget wine is a commodity, and the longer you keep it in the cellar, the longer you tie up capital. An early wine, just like Beaujolais Nouveau, shows the versatility of the grapes, which can produce good wine at many stages and provide income at the earliest stage of a vineyard. (For history buffs, Castello di Borghese made the first young wine in 2002, Novello, from pinot noir grapes. It received a rave review from Howard Goldberg of the *New York Times*.)

Gangl looked at the amount of chardonnay coming in off Macari vines and saw his opportunity. Ten years later the wine is still a hit: low in alcohol, a touch of sweetness with zingy acidity that makes you want to take another sip.

Chardonnay for Early Wine is picked usually about two weeks before chardonnay used to make estate wine. "We want to keep the green apple character," says Urbanik Koch. The fruit is picked, pressed off right away and bottled immediately when there's still some carbon dioxide in the wine, which gives it a bit of a spritz. The wine is pale and at first whiff, many people mistake it for riesling. "It's a great way for people to understand the way wine evolves while it's being made," she adds. "It captures that moment in the fermentation. The sweetness and effervescence." That's the immediate impact. "It's fun to have a taste of the harvest when we're still in harvest."

"I love early wine," says Urbanik Kock. "It's a great expression of chardonnay and not meant to be complicated. It is what it is, not meant to be anything other than perfect for summer. It's like life on the North Fork," she continues. "Laid back, tastes good, goes well with all the local foods, low alcohol so you can have more than one glass. The type of wine I think everyone can like." It also serves as a foil for those who think they don't like chardonnay, she says. "I don't meet a lot of people who don't like it."

This is her fourth season of Early Wine, and Urbanik Koch thinks it's the most balanced yet, with the sweetness and acid playing perfectly against each other. In 2013 the Macaris made 904 cases of Early Wine, and it's usually sold out by the beginning of June, as it should be.

This wine is also special to Urbanik Koch because it was bottled on her wedding day, when she married a man she met while playing volleyball.

"I'm proud of this wine," she says. "I think it's different."

Kareem Massoud: Necessity Is the Mother of Invention

Behind the Bottle: Paumanok Vineyards 1993 Late Harvest Sauvignon Blanc

L ate spring 2014, Kareem Massoud was climbing over new oak barrels with a glass wine thief in one hand, a wine glass in the other and a step stool under his feet that was really too short for the job. There are a lot of hard edges in a barrel room. The barrels themselves are rimmed in metal and the floor is an unforgiving concrete. But there you go, there's another element of a winemaker's job not exactly in the description: multitasking while balancing on the top bar of a stool with only two steps. Massoud was using the thief, a tube with holes on each end, the draw wine for tasting. Once dunking it into a full barrel, Massoud "stole" a few ounces of wine by covering the top hole with his thumb. Moving the thief over his glass, he lifts his thumb and lets the wine, so rich and concentrated it's almost black, slide into his glass. I reach up, offering my glass for a share of the sample. It's not how he spends many of his days, but the promise of some kind of physical labor greets most winemakers every morning: using clumsy equipment (that often breaks down) to move wine from many barrels into a tank to prepare for bottling; backing up a fork lift to heft palettes piled with cases of wine into storage or rolling empty barrels into the yard to be cleaned.

What he was excited about on this day were the 2013 wines—merlot, cabernet franc, and cabernet—aging in the barrels, some new from a French cooperage, Bossuet, he's newly working with, and some a few years old, which impart less oak flavor in the wine. The winemaker at his family's winery, Paumanok Vineyards in Aquebogue, Massoud, the oldest son, joined his father, Charles, in the job in 2001. Since then, 2013 is as fine a vintage as he has seen.

"The wines have such concentration," he says, marveling at the color. "I'd love to leave them in the barrel longer, but as my father says, 'You can't explain aging wine to the bank,'" or leaving them in the cellar too long once bottled, but some wines are kept around for the library and special occasions. For that day, Massoud and I were set to taste Paumanok's 1993 Late Harvest Sauvignon Blanc, a wine made 20 years ago in what some would say is a vintage that rivals 2013. The two vintages followed difficult years: 2012 had the messiness of Superstorm Sandy, which challenged winemakers and growers, who knew the hurricane would make their choice of when to pick for them; and 1992, when the eruption in late 1991 of our old friend Mount Pinatubo coated the skies as far as Long Island with ash and soot creating a growing season in 1992 that other winemakers still refer to as a disaster. From this disaster, the Massoud's late harvest wine was born.

"My parents had just had the winery for nine years and were just beginning to make their own wine," says Massoud. "And my mother was all bent out of shape, because the fruit was beginning to rot. She came to father in tears, saying that we were going to lose the vintage."

Here Massoud recounts his father's response, one that demonstrates his father's no-nonsense demeanor: "He said, 'Let's sleep on it; we'll walk the vineyard tomorrow.' The next morning, in the vineyard he said, 'I don't smell vinegar. That's good.'"

Then Massoud's mother, Ursula, drew upon her experience growing up around vineyards in her native Germany. "My mother was like 'This is Edelfäule!' And my dad said, 'What's

Edelfäule?' They realized they had noble rot on their hands and thought 'Maybe we can do something with this.'"

Noble rot, or Botrytis cinerea, is the gray mold responsible for some of the greatest dessert wines in the world. It creates the golden wines of Sauternes and the rich full-bodied Tokaji Aszu of Hungary. The rot desiccates the grapes from the outside without breaking the skin. What's left is concentrated sweet grape juice and an unreplicable earthy flavor.

In 1992, botrytis affected the Massoud's sauvignon blanc and reisling. A botrysized wine made entirely from sauvignon blanc is rare, especially in the United States, but in Sauternes the wine is made from a combination of sauvignon blanc and sémillon. Sauvignon blanc is a high acid grape, which is necessary to balance the sweetness of the wine.

"You could say it saved the vintage," says Massoud. "If they had decided this was no good and dropped the fruit, it would have been a great loss. It was a remarkable turn of events, and one of the best wines we ever made."

Being a winemaker was not in Kareem Massoud's future growing up in Connecticut with a father who worked for IBM. "But my father got what he calls 'the Bronze Parachute' a buyout deal that enabled him to retire at 49 with the benefits of being 55," he says. "For people like my father, it was a no-brainer; he jumped on it."

In 1983, his parents bought the farm where they still live and planted the first vines that year. In 1990 they converted a potato barn into a winery and moved in full time in 1993 two years after Massoud left home to start at Wharton as an undergrad at the University of Pennsylvania. "I went to Penn thinking I was going to be a businessman," he says. "But by the time I was a junior I wanted to work for my parents." They weren't having it. "They said, 'That's not why we're sending you to an Ivy League college.' They weren't sure the winery was going to make any money." So he went to a private investment firm but worked on weekends and during harvest at the winery. After two years, he quit the investment firm and moved to back home to work full time.

"I feel like I retired 30 or 40 years early," he says. "Because I love what I'm doing, and it was what I was doing on weekends and during vacations anyway."

In the meantime, his parents were busy. They made their first wine, a chardonnay, in 1989 at Bridgehampton Winery, where Richard Olsen-Harbich, now of Bedell, was the wine-maker. The wine ended up on the shelves of Sherry-Lehmann, a high-end wine shop in Manhattan. Soon, noted restaurants like La Caravelle were putting Paumanok wines on their lists.

They started adding more acreage to the original farm's 45. They bought a neglected vineyard across the street, which added 30 more farmable acres and one of the winery's most popular grapes, chenin blanc. The vineyard was in such disrepair that the Massouds had to rip out a bunch of the vines, including some zinfandel. The chenin was almost destined for the compost heap, but a visiting vineyard consultant thought the vines looked happy where they were, and they were saved, another unexpected success.

In 2004, the family was part of a lottery to acquire some land owned by the local power company, a large tract that was once meant to house a nuclear power plant. The Long Island Farm Bureau worked to get the land protected and offered at a good price to working farmers. Names were tumbled in a barrel and a coterie of farmers watched—some had brought their ducks—as names were drawn. The Massouds were plucked first, so they had their pick of the lots, a 29-acre parcel that soon had 25 under vine. "As my father says, it's the only lottery that you have to write a check when you win," says Massoud. In early 2014, the family was working on yet another deal for more land.

One reason the Massouds' name came up so early in the lottery was their commitment to land preservation, says Massoud. To help with the purchase of the original farm, his parents sold the development rights, which guarantees the land will never be turned over to housing. "They wanted to be sure, even if the winery didn't work out, that the land would never be developed," he says. Currently the family owns 101 acres in total.

And they're still making late harvest dessert wine in the years Mother Nature gives them the noble rot. Massoud gently pulls a cork from of the neck of the bottle it's been stopping for 20 years; it's dark and compact. "Isn't that cool? It's 20 years old," he says. Atop the cork was a dime-sized disk of wax. "I was just waxing the top of bottles this morning," he adds as he pours out the amber-colored 1993 Late Harvest Sauvignon Blanc. The wine smells oxidized, like Sherry, but there's still some fruit in the background. "It's definitely past the development stage," he says. "It's an aged wine with that oxidative character, but it still has the richness and complexity it had when it was younger. It's a little bit caramelized.

"It might not be for everyone," he adds, "but for the adventurous, it's still a fun wine." He looks at the half-empty bottle. "And it's easy to drink."

The wine was made by Massoud's father using the same technique he had first used the year before. Botrysized grapes don't look so great when they reach the winery. They're dark and shriveled, about one quarter the size of an unaffected grape. "You look at it and think, 'I'm not going to eat that,'" says Massoud. "But it's like an overripe banana, if you do eat it, it's really delicious and sweet." Once they hit the press—as whole clusters—they turn to mush and release a viscous juice. Charles Massoud had decided to barrel ferment the wine, just as it is done in Sauterne. "We use new Vosges [French] oak barrels," says Massoud. "They're very soft and mellow, without assertive oak flavors. The wine gets all the benefits of a new barrel—open pores that haven't been clogged up yet—but it's not too oaky. You almost can't tell there was oak."

It's true. The wine is more expressive on the palate than on the nose, which is unusual in any wine, and the flavors have melded together beautifully: a touch of vanilla, caramelized sugar and preserved citrus all balanced with a zip of acid that keeps the wine from being too sweet. It'd be hard to identify as sauvignon blanc even with that acid.

The grapes for the wine come from the block directly behind the winery that is overlooked by the deck surrounding the tasting room. Normally the family can pick about three tons per acre from these vines, but when they are affected by noble rot, the yield reduces to as little as a half ton per acre, which is why it is precious. Noble rot cannot be reliably predicted at Paumanok, so the late harvest wine is not made every year, usually only in the cooler vintages. As it has turned out, there's been one about every three years. In 2012, the family decided to pick a little earlier, to increase yield at the expense of super botrysized grapes. It turns out, if they had decided to wait and pick later, the crop would have been lost to Sandy.

Massoud shrugs. Making wine is all about coincidences, serendipity and courting disaster, making lemonade out of lemons and sweet wine out of what looked like a lost cause.

Regan Meador:
The Right Kind of Weird

Behind the Bottles: Southold Farm +
Cellar 2013 Damn the Torpedoes,
a sparkling red blend; 2013 The Devil's
Advocate, old vines chardonnay;
2013 Cast Your Fate to the Wind;
whole-cluster cabernet franc

He seems to have backed off a bit, but Regan Meador got into the wine biz with the clarion call on Kickstarter, "I like weird grapes." To the consternation of a few making Long Island wine, he seemed a little too dismissive of chardonnay and merlot, the two most planted grapes on the East End. (Merlot is also one of the most planted fine wine grapes in the world, so someone must like it.) But sit down with him for a bit and you'll find he doesn't come off as a bomb-throwing revolutionary. He's more of a Generation Y maverick, jumping with both feet into a tub of grapes to see what squeezes out. If you think about it, really, Meador is the next logical step in the evolution of Long Island wine. He knows he is standing on the shoulders of his winemaking forebears, and without their decades of devotion to proving Long Island can make good wine, he may have wound up growing pinot noir in the Anderson Valley. "We don't have the burden these guys had," he says, standing in the homey kitchen of his renovated farmhouse in Southold. "The baggage from slaving away for 20 years or more and only now getting recognition from places they needed that recognition from 10 to 20 years ago." Like for other younger winemakers, such as Anthony Nappa and Kelly Urbanik Koch, the fact people used to turn up their noses at Long Island wine doesn't really resonate. "I know we can make distinctive and great wine," he says, like the obvious statement is obvious.

Meador grew up in west Texas into a ranching family and attended a high school with 700 people in each class. He spent time with his grandfather going to auctions and tending cattle and sheep—and for a short period emus—before leaving for Denver to go to college, where he studied finance. "I had two different jobs in Dallas, but I wanted to be in the music business," he says. So he and a buddy struck out for New York City in 2004. "He had a job, and I was frantically looking for one." He turned to Craig's List and saw an ad for a job in what was yet to be called social media for the comeback tour of Duran Duran. "You know," he says, "it was the time of My Space." That gig led to managing bands and starting a music PR company. "It was a lot of fun," he says. "We went on tours in the UK and played some pretty decent sized shows. But there's no money in that business, and you need money to live in New York." His income cut into his ability to enjoy the Rhone Valley wines had had come to love while working as a banker. "Good wine can be inexpensive," he says, "but I was just getting by. The amount of wine I was able to procure for myself was getting less and less."

His proclivity for marketing was getting better and better, however, so he sucked it up and started at an advertising firm. "I was a strategist, the guy behind the two-way mirror," he says. And at that time a digital marketing background was a hot commodity in advertising. "I worked on Dos Equis and Heineken. I launched the E-Trade baby. It was fun for what it was, but I kind of knew it wasn't a forever career, and I knew New York was not a permanent stop."

In 2007 a friend got a job at a wine shop, "and that reignited everything," says Meador. "From there it just grew. The higher up I got, the more I bought." The following year he met his wife, Carey, who grew up in Cutchogue, and was thus exposed to the Long Island wine business. "We'd come to visit and I'd hit all the wineries," he says. It only served to whet his desire to get out of the city. His tastings drew him to smaller wineries. He remembers being wowed by Eric Fry's work at Lenz and the wines of Roanoke Vineyards. He also has great respect for Urbanik Koch, the winemaker at Macari. "She just wants to make the best wines possible," he says, adding that he thinks many winemakers would shrug at making an early wine, which Urbanik Koch highlighted in her chapter of this book. "They might not want to put their all into it. Winemakers generally want to make serious wine, wine that gets you serious scores, and that's when you become a celebrity winemaker."

The couple started to talk about getting married and raising a family. "I knew I didn't want to live in the city or raise kids in the city, and I didn't want to live in the suburbs," he says. "It was apparent if I stayed in advertising, we would be tied to a city."

So he really started looking at the wine business. *How can I get into it,* he thought. *Was there a marketing angle?* But he didn't really want that either. "I wanted to get my hands dirty," he says. "Being a winemaker is such a nebulous thing; how is it even possible?" He decided it was because people just started doing it. "Like how do you become a movie director," he asks. "You just do it." He decided not to worry about going to school and start at the beginning. All he had to figure out was where to get a job. One option was California, where family members owned that pinot noir vineyard. Texas was an option as was Michigan, where other family members lived.

A visit to winejobs.com in 2011 led him to Adam Suprenant at Osprey's Dominion, who was advertising for help. "I went from having no wine business experience to being an assistant winemaker," he says. "The great thing was it was only me in that cellar with Adam. Every little thing that happened I was doing. As far as an education goes, I don't think I could have gotten any better. Even the kids that go to oenology school, it's not until you're really in it and put it into practice that you learn." (Meador adds that he thinks Suprenant prides himself on hiring complete novices, which he has done four times, because they go straight into his system.)

His ad agency co-workers not only wished him luck, they were jealous. "They said, 'Why can't I do that?'" says Meador. "They wanted to know how I made it happen. It's not rocket science. It's not like I have some winemaking gift. You have to be willing to give up something to do something completely different. Which is really where the whole crux of this lies, in your confidence in yourself. That you'll be able to figure it out."

In the meantime, he and Carey got married in April 2011; she was completely supportive of the change and ended up keeping her job in the city commuting in a few days a week. Three months later, Meador moved in with her parents and started at Osprey's Dominion. Meador was sold. "Right out of the gate I was totally happy with the work," he says. "When you've spent the last 10 years sitting behind a desk, dealing with people and writing PowerPoint presentations, you kind of lose touch. There's something really human about be able to work with your hands."

The next year the couple bought their current farm, which included a derelict farmhouse and 23.7 acres of land, and set to the work of renovating, with a large amount of help from Steve O'Connor, Carey's dad, who is a retired electrician with a plumbing license. "He's what made the construction thing possible," says Meador. "Between his knowledge and the Internet, we were able build."

The house, originally a saltbox built in the mid-1800s and expanded with lean-tos, was part of a parcel bought in 2005 by Leucadia, a Manhattan-based investment firm with ties to Napa Valley. The company's purchase, which got many in the industry and local press excited about the influx of big names and money in wine country, came to naught. They ripped up existing vineyards—Broadfields and Charles John—and then left town. The property lay fallow for the next seven years.

After two seasons at Osprey's, Meador moved to Lenz for the 2013 vintage. Soon the house was finished, he started the Kickstarter that raised $24,900, and he was ready to plant some weird grapes. In went three acres of lagrein, two and a half of teroldego, both native to the northeast of Italy; two of syrah and one acre of goldmuskateller, the German name for the gold muscat grape of the Alto Adige. "My father-in-law and I pounded every single one of those post," he says. The same year he bought chardonnay from Steve Mudd, which turned into his Devil's Advocate; merlot, petite verdot and cab franc from Rex Farr, an organic winegrower in Riverhead in the western reaches of the East End; and pinot noir from Sheldrake, a winery in the Finger Lakes.

If he couldn't use his weird grapes, he was going to make the wine in a weird way, using his experience at Osprey's and Lenz and his knowledge from reading up on winemaking. "I understand how the science works," he says. "And while I don't have a lot of the super technical stuff, that'll just happen over time. I feel like some of that, the chemistry, can be navel gazing." He also believes being an owner/operator is the best way to succeed, citing the examples of Kip Bedell, the couple David Page and Barbara Shinn of Shinn Estate Vineyards and the Massoud Family of Paumanok. Cautionary tales, like the recent closing of Peconic Bay Winery, a very popular place, loom large in his mind. "I see what these wineries have to turn into the support themselves. It becomes less about the wine and more about the experience." He adds, "It's not to say that I don't think there shouldn't be big wineries. Paumanok's not small, but it's also not a tourism spot; there's not a lot of fluff going on. They're just making and selling wine, good wine."

Meador brought his grapes to Raphael in Peconic, where friend Anthony Nappa is the winemaker, and began his experiment. The first was the Devil's Advocate made with the chardonnay from Mudd's 40-year-old vines. Those plants are unique because they're a musque clone, which is rarely planted anymore on the East End. Just as it sounds, the wine made from it has a musky quality and is more aromatic than clones from California and the Dijon clones local winemakers rely on today. What Meador was going for was almost the opposite of the style of chardonnay that is popular now, which is invariably made without oak and with an emphasis on acid. The pressed grapes were left on the skins for a week before the juice was put to ferment in large new oak barrels that had been washed with some of Nappa's wine to rinse out the oak flavors. The size of the barrels—230 gallons, nearly four times the size of a standard barrel—also limited the wine's exposure to oak. Once the juice filled the barrels in October, Meador left it alone until March. No addition of yeast and no stirring of the lees. Sulfur dioxide was added as a preservative just before bottling.

"When I went in to make it, I didn't know how I was going to feel about it," he says. "I don't like big oaky flabby wines, but I knew I had to go that route to get the aromatics out. I've also gotten so that I don't like those crispy stainless steel wines anymore. I want something with a little weight to it."

Weight it does have, as well as the scent of a more aromatic grape like viognier, with apricot and a little spice. One would be hard pressed to immediately identify it as chardonnay. It almost has the oily texture of viognier, which can be high in alcohol; I would drink it at room temperature—to heighten the aromatics—with heavier food, almost like a red wine.

Meador also made a cabernet franc, using grapes from the Farrm, Rex Farr's vineyard, but he used a variant of carbonic maceration, a technique dominant in Beaujolais. The idea is to leave the grapes in whole clusters until they start to ferment from the inside out. The result is a highly aromatic wine with typical aromas of cinnamon and bubble gum. This wine, which Meador calls Cast Your Fate to the Wind, nails that aroma profile so precisely it's like sticking your nose in a candy jar. Despite the perceived sweetness on the nose, the wine is completely dry with astringent tannins that wipe the wetness from your tongue. "I was looking at cru Beaujolais and wondered what would happen if I used their technique with cab franc," he says. "I think the best iterations I've had of cab franc haven't been in a big masculine style. I hate cab francs that don't remind you they're cab francs." For our tasting, Meador also poured some of the wine from a bottle of Cast Your Fate to the Wind that had been open for five days. The cinnamon and bubble gum are still there, but the vegetal character typical of cab franc character comes through. And the tannins had mellowed a bit, so were no longer as drying.

His third wine released in 2014 is a sparkling red made with merlot, petit verdot and pinot noir. The grapes were pressed and vinified at Raphael and then driven upstate to Bellwether Cidery, where the wine was pressurized in a tank and bottled, using a counter pressure bottling line, to save all the fizz. The wine is called Damn the Torpedoes and was modeled after dry lambrusco, a wine native to the Emilia-Romagna region of Italy, where fatty meats and ricotta filled tortelloni are culinary staples. "I've always been a fan of lambrusco, and I wanted to make something you could drink in the summer out here that was a red wine," says Meador. "On a summer night when I'm grilling a steak, a big red wine is not something I want to drink. And I'm not going to replace it with chardonnay."

The wine has bright berry flavors and a dusty smell with prickly bubbles and light dusty tannins. "It's certainly not a varietal wine," he says. "I liken it more to blending, a chef's style of making wine where I'm creating something rather than showing off terrior." While light in body, the wine still has the depth of a red wine and will stand up to decanting. "It evolves like crazy over a dinner or a night," he says. "I wish I had the luxury that Eric [Fry at Lenz] has to let things sit in bottle for two years before selling it, but at the end of the day, this is a business."

The grapes from his own vineyard won't be ready to make wine for the next one or two years, so Meador intends to keep buying all the grapes Rex Farr grows and making wine in different styles. "I might make a cab franc rosé next year or a Bordeaux style wine with heavy maceration," he says. "I think it would be interesting to make wine from the same vineyard every year, but with a different technique and discover the terrior through that."

He was lucky to have 2013 as his inaugural vintage; it was a growing season Long Island will be taking about for years, when an extremely dry fall produced masses of pristine grapes. "I think these wines set the tone of what we're planning to do here," he says. "For a rookie, I got a pretty good vintage to start out with. But I plan to let the vineyard dictate what I make. I'm not trying to emulate any one region. I'm trying to explore in different ways what is possible."

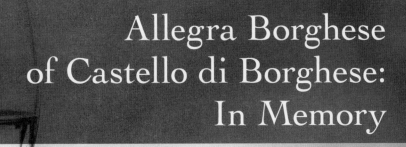

Allegra Borghese
of Castello di Borghese:
In Memory

Behind the Bottle:
Castello di Borghese Allegra

J ust like most girls, Allegra Borghese wanted a big Sweet 16 party. Her parents, Ann Marie and Marco, the owners of Castello di Borghese in Cutchogue on the North Fork, said no. The disappointment did not last too long. That year, the winery released a dessert wine for the first time, a late harvest riesling they named Allegra.

"Now," says Borghese, "ten years later, it's way cooler than having a party. Sometimes we have events and people ask me to sign the bottles."

Ten years later, her attitude is not the only thing that changed. Borghese and her brothers have taken over their parents' winery after losing their mother to cancer and their father to a car accident within one horrible week in June 2014.

At age 26 Borghese is learning how to run a business that includes fixing glass washers, managing employees, and organizing events in addition to the work that ends up producing wine. Fortunately, the staff has stayed on, and vineyard management and wine making will continue to be supervised by Bernard Ramis with help from consulting winemaker Eric Bilka.

Like many who visit the East End of Long Island for the first time, Ann Marie and Marco were impressed by the region's beauty, fertility and wine. A family friend drove the couple around, and one stop was in Cutchogue at Hargrave Vineyard, the first commercially planted vineyard with French wine grapes on Long Island, which was for sale. "My dad asked how much," says Allegra. "And my mom thought it was for a bottle, but it was for the winery."

That was 1998. Two years later the family moved from Philadelphia and Allegra started at the public school in Mattituck. Her oldest brother, Fernando, had already moved out; her other brother, Giovanni, went to boarding school.

The transition, she says, was difficult for her and her mother. "We're city girls." So Allegra finished high school early and went on to earn a graduate degree in counseling and art therapy, which she finished in the fall after her parents' deaths, a circumstance that altered her plans for the future.

"Right now there's no choice," she says. "My brothers and I are running the winery. I feel like I have a responsibility—to the people who work here—and an opportunity. How many 26-year-olds can say they're running a business?"

It's a business uniquely tied to her parents.

Marco was the face and voice of the winery. An Italian nobleman by birth, his accented sonorous voice was as distinguishable as it was warm. Ann Marie hosted vineyard walks and was a presence at the local farmers markets where she poured her wine for shoppers, appearances she made until a short time before her death. Few knew she was sick.

"I feel like I'm much more intimately aware of the day to day of my parents," says Allegra. "I'm sitting at my father's desk and driving my mother's car. I'm in their psychological space. And now I can better understand why they were the way were. It's chilling." She pauses and smiles. "But in a good way."

At her feet is Brix, her mother's Italian pointer, a constant presence in the tasting room and companion in the office. He doesn't let Allegra out of his sight.

Since her parents' deaths, Allegra has been working mostly with her brother Giovanni, who has taken on the tasks his mother used to handle, while Allegra stays at the winery. The two did spend time while growing up helping out. Allegra pitched in, hanging art shows and preparing for events; Giovanni, she says, got tossed on the bottle line when he was being punished. While their experiences were not their main work activities, the winery—and its wine—was a big part of their lives.

"I love food and wine pairing and coming up with creative terms to describe the wine," she says. "It's a very seductive business; it has that lure of excitement and can feel fun." She pauses and lights up with a big smile. "I love wine, and I happen to really like the wines we produce. I'm genuinely proud of our product and I'm very picky about my wines. You can call me a wine snob. I'm proud of that."

The wine lineup at Borghese is similar to most Long Island wineries: chardonnay, sauvignon blanc, riesling, merlot, some pinot noir, cabernet franc and cabernet sauvignon. The vineyard boasts some of the oldest vines on Long Island, planted by the Hargraves in 1973.

"We're the first and the finest, and we're proud of that," says Allegra. She is proud of their pinot noir, which she says is their best grape. A recent success from them has been white pinot noir. But her favorite wine is the Meritage, a red blend made in the best years. The Allegra is now made from chardonnay.

Outside, in the vineyard she finds some solace in the wake of the adjustments necessary after such a large loss, in front of great new responsibility and the present challenge of learning to work well with her siblings. "We can listen to each other," she says. "It's a good skill, but we can get angry at the each other. It's hard because it's conflated our parents' loss and the running of a company."

That's when a walk among the vines is helpful. "We also get to have an open relationship with nature," she says. "It's interesting to have a lifestyle that really depends on the weather. It's such a beautiful landscape; I can look out and know it's all ours. It makes the days less stressful. It makes the broken machine days feel more balanced."

Beyond fixing machines and selling the next bottles, Allegra and her brothers aren't making far-reaching plans. She says the winery is making money and she is confident her parents are watching her in awe, with pride.

"They're just spectators, going along with what I do next," she says. "I just think they want me to be happy. They never wanted me to fit a certain mold, never wanted me to do something out of a place of duty or to please them. But I really do want to make them proud; I really do want to please them, and this is the way to do that."

Acknowledgments

Writing about wine is a dream job; there's no doubt about it. Visiting beautiful vineyards and aromatic wine cellars is so pleasurable and interesting that I almost forget the work of getting the words down on the page. Almost.

This task is made easier by the people at the wineries. And for this book, each one I met with had stories and wine and, most importantly, the time to tell me all I needed to know. For that I am grateful, because a wine region is nothing without the people who make it run. In *Behind the Bottle*, I focused on winemakers and a few winegrowers, but everything I've learned in the 12 years I've been living in and writing about Long Island Wine Country has come from participants in the whole business and the Long Island Wine Council, which brings it all together. Thanks to everyone—including chefs, farmers and fishermen—for making me part of the region. I hope you see how much I appreciate it in the preceding pages.

Speaking of making things easy, I thank Carlo DeVito for initiating this project and connecting me with the people at Cider Mill Press: publisher John Whalen Jr., publishing manager Alexandra Lewis, designer Alicia Freile, cover designer Whitney Cookman, and editor Amy Paradysz. They guided me with a firm hand and introduced me to book publishing, which varies greatly from my world of magazines.

That world would not exist without the intrepid founders of *Edible East End* magazine. Since 2005, Brian Halweil and Stephen Munshin have given me a venue not only to explore the food and wine of the East End of Long Island but have employed me to do so. I am proud to have been a part of it.

In the process I have been able to use my education at International Wine Center, where I earned a diploma in wine and spirits under the tutelage of Mary Ewing-Mulligan MW and Linda Lawry. Mary was kind enough to write the Foreword for this book. She is the first woman in the United States to become a Master of Wine; it's a big deal and I am very grateful.

None of the above would have happened without my mother, who died in 2013 before I started this book. She would have gotten such a kick out of it. I thank her for always being my number-one fan.

And thanks to my dog Ukie. Despite his insistence on sitting on my lap, I was still able to type.

Index

List of Winemakers and Wineries

Rich Olsen-Harbich of Bedell Cellars
2010 Taste Red
36225 Main Road
Cutchogue, NY 11935
Phone: 631-734-7537
Fax: 631-734-5788
Website: www.bedellcellars.com
Email: wine@bedellcellars.com

Eric Fry of The Lenz Winery
1997 & 2007 Old Vines Merlot
38355 Main Road
Peconic, NY 11958
Phone: 631-734-6010
Website: www.lenzwine.com
Email: office@lenzwine.com

Roman Roth
Wölffer Estate 1997 Estate Selection Chardonnay; 2012
White Mischief (chardonnay); Grapes of Roth 2008 Merlot;
2005 Christian Cuvée (merlot blend)
139 Sagg Road
P.O. Box 9002
Sagaponack, NY 11962
Phone: 631-537-5106
Fax: 631-537-5107
Website: www.wolffer.com
Email: info@wolffer.com

Russell Hearn
1994 & 1995 Encore, Pellegrini's red blend
23005 Route 25
Cutchogue, NY 11935
Phone: 631-734-4111
Fax: 631-734-4159
Website: www.pellegrinivineyards.com
Email: wine@pellegrinivineyards.com

Miguel Martin of Palmer Vineyards
2010 Old Roots Merlot
5120 Sound Avenue, Route 48
Riverhead, NY 11901
Phone: 631-722-WINE (9463)
Fax: 631-722-5364
Website: www.palmervineyards.com
Email: tastinghouse@palmervineyards.com

Gilles Martin of Sparkling Pointe
Sparkling Pointe 2005 Brut Seduction
39750 Route 48
Southold, NY 11935
Phone: 631-765-0200
Website: www.sparklingpointe.com
Email: info@sparklingpointe.com

Anthony Nappa of Anthony Nappa Wines
Anomaly vertical
Phone: 774-641-7488
Website: www.anthonynappawines.com
Email: info@anthonynappawines.com
Tasting Room:
The Winemaker Studio
2885 Peconic Lane Peconic, NY 11958

Adam Suprenant of Coffee Pot Cellars
2008 Coffee Pot Cellars Merlot
Tasting Room
31855 Main Road
Cutchogue, NY 11935
Phone: 631-765-8929
Website: www.coffeepotcellars.com
Email: tastingroom@coffeepotcellars.com

Barbara Shinn
Shinn Vineyards
2000 Oregon Road
Mattituck, NY 11952
Phone: 631-804-0367
Fax: 631-298-0216
Website: www.shinneestatevineyards.com
Email: info@shinnestatevineyards.com

Larry Perrine and James Christopher Tracy
of Channing Daughters
2012 & 2007 Vino Bianco; 2012 Lagrein
1927 Scuttlehole Road
P.O. Box 2202
Bridgehampton, NY 11932
Phone: 631-537-7224
Website: www.channingdaughters.com
Email: info@channingdaughters.com

Ron Goerler Jr.
Jamesport Vineyards
1997 Merlot and 2001 Cabernet Franc
1216 Main Road, Route 25
P.O. Box 842
Jamesport, NY 11947
Phone: 631-722-5256
Fax: 631-722-5256
Website: www.jamesportwines.com
Email: jamesportvineyards@msn.com

Kelly Urbanik Koch of Macari Vineyards
2013 Early Wine
150 Bergen Ave.
P.O. Box 2
Mattituck, NY 11952
Tastings: 11 a.m. to 5 p.m. daily
Phone: 631-298-0100
Fax: 631-298-8373
Website: www.macariwines.com
Email: info@macariwines.com

Kareem Massoud of Paumanok Vineyards
1992 Late Harvest Sauvignon Blanc
1074 Main Road
Aquebogue, NY 11931
Website: www.paumanok.com
Email: info@paumanok.com

Regan Meador of Southold Farm+Cellar
2013 Damn the Torpedoes, 2013 The Devil's Advocate,
and 2013 Cast Your Fate to the Wind
860 Old North Road, Southold, NY 11971
Phone: 631-353-0343
Website: www.southoldfarmandcellar.com/
Email: info@southoldfarmandcellar.com

Allegra Borghese of Castello di Borghese
Allegra Dessert Wine
17150 County Route 48
P.O. Box 957
Cutchogue, NY 11935
Phone: 631-734-5111
Website: www.castellodiborghese.com
Email: info@castellodiborghese.com

About Cider Mill Press

Good ideas ripen with time. From seed to harvest, Cider Mill Press brings fine reading, information, and entertainment together between the covers of its creatively crafted books. Our Cider Mill bears fruit twice a year, publishing a new crop of titles each spring and fall.

Visit us on the Web at
www.cidermillpress.com
or write to us at
12 Spring Street PO Box 454
Kennebunkport, Maine 04046